Bat 6

with Connections

Bat 6

Virginia Euwer Wolff

with
Connections

HOLT, RINEHART AND WINSTON

A Harcourt Classroom Education Company

Austin · New York · Orlando · Atlanta · San Francisco · Boston · Dallas · Toronto · London

For Sarah Wolff Hamel

Thanks to: Marilyn E. Marlow, Anthony Wolff, Juliet Wolff, Gene and Meg Euwer, Linny and Dennis Stovall, Don Gallo, Sue Macy, Mary Spangenberg, Mary Jo Wade, Cheryl Acheson, Lawson Fusao Inada, Katharine Ballash, Takako Ebisawa, Nancy Moller, Mary Gunesch, Bill Gunesch, Laura Godwin, Grace Chen, M.D., Mark Harris, Barry Varela, the Rev. Ashley M. Cook, the Rev. Nan Geer, Bill Plummer III of the Amateur Softball Association, the National Softball Hall of Fame, the National Baseball Hall of Fame, the Oregon City Pioneers and Coach Will Rhinehart, the Oregon City Babes and Coach Rick Snyder, Spalding Sports Worldwide, Wilson Sporting Goods, Sears Merchandise Group, the staff of the Gladstone Public Library; and, feather by feather, to Brenda Bowen.

Contents

Author's Note

Softball became an official sport in 1933. Before that year, the game had been called kitten ball, ladies' baseball, and soft baseball, and had had widely differing rules. The Amateur Softball Association published the first standardized rules in 1934.

The Japanese navy bombed Pearl Harbor on December 7, 1941.

On February 19, 1942, President Franklin Delano Roosevelt signed Executive Order 9066, ordering the evacuation and imprisonment for the duration of World War II of all persons of Japanese ancestry living in the western United States.

Ten camps were hastily built in order to house the thousands of families who were to be removed from their homes. The camps were scattered: Tule Lake and Manzanar in California; Minidoka in Idaho; Topaz in Utah; Poston and Gila River in Arizona; Heart Mountain in Wyoming; Granada in Colorado; Rohwer and Jerome in Arkansas. The total number of men, women, and children interned in the camps from 1942 to 1945 was 120,113.

Not until 1952 were *Issei,* Japanese-Americans born in Japan, permitted to become U.S. citizens.

In 1987, the United States Supreme Court declared the internment of Japanese-Americans unconstitutional, calling it "one of the worst violations of civil liberties in American history." The United States government officially apologized to all American citizens of Japanese ancestry in 1988.

THE FIFTIETH ANNIVERSARY BAT 6
MAY 28, 1949
BEAR CREEK RIDGE GRADE SCHOOL TEAM ROSTER

PITCHER	**Shadean**	Bats right, throws right
CATCHER	**Tootie**	Bats right, throws left and right
FIRST BASE	**Aki**	Bats left, throws left
SECOND BASE	**Kate**	Bats right, throws right
SHORTSTOP	**Ellen**	Bats right, throws right
THIRD BASE	**Daisy (Loose Lips)**	Bats right, throws right
RIGHT FIELD	**Little Peggy**	Bats left and right, throws right
CENTER FIELD	**Lorelei**	Bats right, throws right
LEFT FIELD	**Susannah**	Bats right, throws right
MANAGER AND GENERAL SUB	**Vernell**	Bats right, throws right

COACH: **MRS. PORTER**

ASSISTANT COACH: **MR. PORTER**

THE FIFTIETH ANNIVERSARY BAT 6
MAY 28, 1949
BARLOW ROAD GRADE SCHOOL TEAM ROSTER

PITCHER	**Ila Mae**	Bats right, throws right and left
CATCHER	**Audrey**	Bats right, throws right
FIRST BASE	**Wink**	Bats right, throws left
SECOND BASE	**Brita Marie**	Bats right, throws right
SHORTSTOP	**Alva**	Bats right, throws right
THIRD BASE	**Darlene**	Bats right, throws right
RIGHT FIELD	**Beautiful Hair Hallie**	Bats right, throws left
CENTER FIELD	**Shazam**	Bats right and left, throws right and left
LEFT FIELD	**Manzanita**	Bats right, throws right
MANAGER AND GENERAL SUBS	**Lola and Lila**	Lola bats right, throws right; Lila bats right, throws left

COACH: **MR. RAYFIELD**

ASSISTANT COACH: **DOTTY RAYFIELD**, MVP 1940

Tootie, Ellen, and Lorelei

Tootie, catcher

ow that it's over, we are telling. We voted to, it's fairer than not. We're all taking our turns, even the ones who don't want to speak up. I'm going first because I was first, sort of. Even though it's hard to tell exactly when it began. I mean exactly when. It began so many different places.

There were some sayings everybody knew: "Come fall, hit that ball." "Mt. Hood gets the first new snow, team positions you have to know." And "Decoration Day, ready to play." Even the old men who sit on McHenrys' Store porch would tell you that.

When I walked past them to buy my new 3-ring binder for 6th grade, one of those men said to me, "Your year, right, Tootie?" They kidded me: "I can smell them hot dogs already." "You gonna hit one over the Barlow fence, Tootie?"

They gave me advice, too. "Keep your legs limber, you never know when a leg'll cramp up on you."

They are the retired Blue brothers and Vernell's mother's old cousin, and they knew I was going to be catcher for our team. They couldn't not know. They had seen me across the road on the school playing field many times in the summer, very often Shadean and me were there practicing. She'd pitch to me and we had very good signals all ready for our game.

It was a rule that official softball team practices couldn't begin till the first day of school of the 6th grade year. But there was no rule that we couldn't be ready. And we were getting ready. The school principal let me borrow the catcher's mask and pads for the summer, like she said, "so you don't kill yourself before you even get to *play* your game, Tootie! For heaven's sake!"

We thought it would be the year of our lives. For 49 years the game had been played between Bear Creek Ridge and Barlow, girls only. It was like just yesterday we were little kids, watching the big girls play their game every spring. May 28, 1949, would be the 50th anniversary game. And we would get to play it.

People were already calling us the 50-year girls.

And I'd made my discovery, and she was going to make all the difference.

I'd discovered Aki. And her champion mother, too. I found Aki by surprise at my summer job in Hirokos' strawberry patch. There she was, a Japanese girl looking about my age, quite a fast berrypicker, nimble you could say, and when I looked up and saw her heave a rotten berry left-handed over into the woods, I said to myself, There's an *arm*.

Right away I thought of our Bat 6 game.

I said to her across the three berry rows between us, "What's your name?" and she said, "Aki," and I said, "My name's Tootie, do you know how to play ball?" and she said, "Yes, I played a lot of it." At lunchtime we played a little bit of catch with my ball I often had with me, and she was right. She was *so* right. She could catch anything. We had no gloves or anything. She's a lefty.

I got home and told my folks about this new girl that just suddenly turned up in the middle of the berry patch, and I said her name, and my mother whirled around from the corn she was shucking and she said, "Aki! That's Aki Mikami — the Mikamis are back?"

You might ask why would my mother not already know the Mikamis were back in such a small country town like ours. Well, that is a long story.

The short part of the story is my mother got on the phone with Susannah's mother and Shadean's mother and Little Peggy's mother, and she even included Lorelei's mother, and they arranged to have a luncheon as a welcoming-back party in honor of Aki's mother, Keiko Mikami. They had a corsage for Mrs. Mikami from Little Peggy's mother's garden, and Mrs. Mikami was so embarrassed she almost didn't say anything at all, and all the mothers agreed she didn't have to say much, it was just good luck and thanks to God she and her family came back.

Aki and I didn't even recognize each other. Even though we used to play together when we were little tiny kids. There is even a picture of Susannah and Aki and me in my mother's album. We were around 2 years old and it was somebody's birthday. But the Mikamis had been away so long.

The truth about Aki and her family is sad. They used to live here. Then every single Japanese had to go to a camp to live because Japan had bombed Pearl Harbor. Even the ones born in America, American citizens. Aki and her brother and even her dad are that. The government sent them to a camp in the desert, and they stayed there for the whole war. They just disappeared, and we were so little nobody explained it to us.

So we didn't know anything about Aki. We went through our grades, from first up to nearly beginning sixth, without knowing she even existed.

And then suddenly her whole family came back.

Hubba hubba ding ding, you should have seen Aki on a ball field. All we had for her was an old ratty glove, the only one for lefties in the sports cupboard. She's very short, but her stretch was great. Lefty is excellent for first base, which I suggested her to be. And you put a bat in her hands, she could hit nearly over to McHenrys' store from the ball field at school, all the way across the road, that's how far. Most girls can't do that. She could hit hard grounders, too.

And I had done a research. By listening in at the luncheon when I was getting ready the cups and saucers. The ladies started talking about it, remembering all those years ago. When I told the girls what I overheard, they were amazed.

"Guess who was MVP in Bat 6 for 1930," I said. Everybody looked blank at me. "Well, she's somebody related to somebody," I hinted. Still nobody got it. "It's Keiko Ishigo, which was Aki's mother before she married Mr. Mikami and had Aki, that's who," I said. They stopped their blank looks and we agreed we might have an MVP standing right there among us.

Aki was embarrassed about it. "Oh, I'm not that good," she said. That's Aki's way. She would rather die than brag.

But she was that good, and everybody including Aki knew it.

Ellen, shortstop

Tootie wouldn't say this herself, but she's a good hitter, she always did like batting a ball, even when others of us wanted to play other things, house or dolls or store or Red Rover.

It was only in sixth grade we all had to pay attention to softball.

When Mrs. Porter was setting up our team with her assistant coach, who was her gorgeous husband named Mr. Porter, she said how lucky we were to have such good equipment, "not like when we came back after the war," she said. She was very proud she was a WAC. The principal was so proud of Mrs. Porter, she put a photograph of her in uniform right up front in the display case of the school. Right beside the Trophy Bats from Bat 6 and the spelling bee plaques that Susanna's father and Aki's father won in 1924. "No new equipment had been made for the duration, the balls were practically shredded, the gloves were nearly in tatters, the bats were scratched and chipped —" I stopped listening to her.

We were so tired of hearing about it. War this, war that. It was over, but not according to the adults that kept talking about it. I'm glad to never see a ration book again in my life.

We all *knew* how bad it was. Everybody suffered. We couldn't help seeing the gold stars in people's windows. And the limping men. Even gorgeous Mr. Porter has a part of his arm missing from being with General Patton. Everybody had a hard time. And the grownups wouldn't stop talking about it.

I had to go away to a completely different school because my dad went in the service and my mom worked in the shipyards in Portland. We lived near the shipyards and I didn't come back here till 4th grade.

In first grade, when I left, nobody was being nice to

Lorelei because of the terrible thing about her father. He wouldn't fight in the war, he doesn't believe in war of any kind. So he had to go to the conscientious-objector camp for the whole duration and do reforestation. People were so nasty to Lorelei and her mother, just on account of how the war came between everybody.

Even by 6th grade, we still felt guilty about Lorelei and we were always nice to her. Even sometimes we were too nice, trying to make up. And Daisy's father still wouldn't speak to Lorelei's father, although Daisy herself was grown up enough to be nice to Lorelei. It was because Daisy's father fought for his country and he hated those that did not.

There was the problem of Daisy, too. In first grade at Sharing Time, she tried to tell where her father was going in the war and Herby shouted very mean, "Loose lips sink ships!" and children began calling Daisy Loose Lips. It is a mean nickname that has hung around all these many years. Even I myself have said it. It's hard to resist, I confess. And it was ridiculous to even think of it. Nobody in our first grade was a spy for the Nazis.

And then there was Aki and her whole family that had to go away. The government ordered them to go. We completely lost track of Aki, we even forgot about her, because the grownups never mentioned the camp.

See why we were so tired of hearing how bad the war was? It just made more bad feelings and we wanted to have our regular girlhood like we deserved.

But they kept reminding me the war was why I have my own bedroom plus the INDOOR BATHROOM in our house from the G.I. loan to my dad. If we didn't have a war, I would not have my own room and it is so beautiful with two windows and even a closet. And the INDOOR BATHROOM is so good you can't even imagine how different. I'll never put my fanny on a cold splintery privy seat again in my whole life. I hope. And I can lie down completely all the way in the brand-new bathtub. It is luxury.

So the war was good. But the war was not good.

I just wanted to stop hearing about it.

What was best about being in sixth grade was team practice. Sometimes it was so funny, like when Tootie got a hit she always said, "See you later!" taking off for first base. Even when we were tired, there were funny things. There was the time Lorelei hit a ball that went way under the huge dogwood tree by the school door, and two of the town dogs sleeping there lurched and started barking to protect the school from it. I can still see the whole bunch of us laughing together. Even now.

Lorelei, center field

"Feel the heft of the bat in your hands, girls." This was Mr. Porter talking, Mrs. Porter our coach's assistant, he was a nifty coach for he made sense about how to do things. He was saying Little Peggy needed to know exactly what weight of bat to use for her size. He was also saying she needed to know where to hold her bat, not choke up too much. "You can even spread your hands a little bit if that feels better. Ty Cobb did. Try it and find what feels right."

It was such a good autumn in a lot of ways. For one thing, there was Aki. I felt such a relief that she came back and she made two of us that were different. I didn't stick out so much anymore. For instance, I had to miss some team practices to go home right after school to pick pears and then apples so they wouldn't ripen too fast on the trees and be ruined. And Aki had to do the same thing, even more so, she had to miss some whole days of school to pick. She did her homework anyway, and I don't think she ever missed a word on a spelling test.

Everybody else was more or less regular and normal but us two. Well, not exactly. Little Peggy was so undersize. And Vernell with her wandering mind. But everybody else was all the same.

Well, there was Susannah. She was a little bit different, to my mind anyway. She had invited me to her seventh birthday party. I had not had a friend the whole first grade. And at her party the girls started to let me be their friend even though their parents were angry at my father. All these years later, Susannah's mother still calls me her special friend, she knew my feelings when I walked in the door to that birthday party when I had not been invited to any other parties. She had secretly made Susannah invite me to her party, although nobody has ever said that in so many words.

Even by 6th grade, Daisy's father would not speak to my father. He walked right past him in McHenrys' Store, acting as if my dad was invisible.

Daisy and I were buddies, doing reports together, sharing lunches, doing eraser and wastebasket duty in partners. She felt terrible about her father. But he is her father. And you have to love your father.

It was so strange about both our fathers, both believing their beliefs so hard they made it into their life. Others had softer beliefs. Like the election. People got angry for Truman or Dewey, but Democrats went right along with the Republicans in everyday things. Being neighbors, selling eggs and goats to each other. It was not such a serious ordeal is what I mean. But Daisy's dad and mine, they would not give an inch.

It was because of my dad I had to miss practices to pick fruit. It was because pickers would hear that my dad didn't fight in the war and they wouldn't come to our place to work. So we didn't have enough workers, and my mom and dad and I had to do a lot of the picking. That's a lot of acres. I missed so many practices.

The worst part was carrying the ladder around, it was so heavy. And the picking bag dug into my shoulders. I took a long hot bath at night, but still.

What happened when my dad's tractor broke down and Shadean's father helped him out, it made my mom cry with gratefulness. The tractor just died right there in the apple rows and we didn't have the money for the repair. And Shadean's dad drove past on his way home from River Bend and he saw our tractor sitting there late at night. He knew something was wrong and he called my dad on the phone to find out what.

And the brand-new baby pear trees were waiting to be planted. My dad would have planted them months before, but we didn't have the money to buy them from the nursery. Then when he did buy them the tractor broke down before he could cultivate the ground.

And then Shadean's father volunteered to bring his brand-new John Deere to pull the cultivator. And sure enough, he got the two acres cultivated out of the goodness of his heart. Not only he cultivated, he said to my dad, "Let's get these trees planted so they don't lose more growth time."

They had my mom and me in charge of the string line to get the rows straight, and in just a few afternoons every little skinny baby pear tree was in the ground. It would have taken us more than double the time without the help.

My mom gave Shadean's mom 3 quarts of mincemeat she made with the venison from the year before's deer and also 2 quarts of crabapple pickles, but she knew such meager food is no adequate payment for such neighborliness in time of need.

Brita Marie, Audrey, Shazam, and Ila Mae

Brita Marie, second base

It was the first day of school, a sunshiny, teeth-chattering September morning. I saw that girl, even before I got to the bike rack.

The first thing I noticed was her high brown shoes with laces up them. Those were not shoes for a girl, they were shoes for a boy and they had been polished real shiny and there was her white socks sticking out over the high tops. Those shoes were awful.

I remembered them from somewhere, and it came to me they were at the Gospel Church rummage sale and ladies were remarking how good they still were, they had lots of wear left. They were saying it was sad how they had belonged to that boy that had to move away when his father went to jail. Those shoes came from McHenrys' Store up on Bear Creek Ridge, they were nearly brand-new.

And it was her dress also. It was a real odd dress for a child to wear, bright red with those big flowers on it. It looked like it had started to be something else, a curtain or a tablecloth. It had buttons all completely down the front and a round ruffled collar. The dress looked like somebody worked hard making it, it was not a store-bought one.

I had the thought in my mind to wave a magic wand and make that new girl not have to be so new. There is no magic wand, and a new girl always has to be her unfamiliar self till somebody takes her in with conversation.

She was holding a spiral notebook and a pencil down to the side of her. She didn't even know we had to have a 3-ring.

I parked my bike next to Beautiful Hair's red one and I took my new 3-ring binder out of the basket, and my brand-new ruler and pencils, and I walked over there to where she was standing, next to the blue spruce tree near the flagpole. Somebody had to take that new girl to another place to stand, because she was in the ornery 6th-grade boys' place.

I said, "Hi, you can come with me, what grade are you in?"

And I will not forget how she answered me: "Shazam. That's my name. They won't have it on their list, they'll have Shirley but you call me Shazam."

"You mean Captain Marvel's Shazam? The magic lightning?" I said.

"Right. Shazam." It was not exactly how she looked new, it was more how she looked different. She was a contrast to us.

And I told her my name, Brita Marie.

"Brita Marie," she said.

"Shazam," I said. We looked straight across into each other's face. "I bet you're in 6th," I said. I didn't have any other hunch from looking at her, only just that one.

"You bet right," she said.

I noticed she had steel eyes.

I wished I could cover up her shoes and her dress for her. She would have to go through 6 hours in that outfit. We walked away from the spruce tree, me with my new blue and yellow skirt and her with that clothing.

I did what I thought was best, I took her over where some of the other girls were, between the flagpole and the blackberry tangle. Darlene, Wink, Audrey, and Beautiful Hair Hallie were there. They tried not to look at her wrong dress and they said hello very friendly. She announced her odd name and Wink asked her did she like to play ball. For 49 years before us there was the famous Bat 6 game of the 6th-grade girls in the springtime, it was a tradition, and Wink naturally had it on her mind. Wink is our exceedingly tall first baseman, her heighth is 5 foot 10 inches.

Shazam stared up at her tallness. "Man, I sure do, ball is what I like to play. You gimme a bat, I'll show you. You gimme a glove, I'll show you," she said.

That reply of hers was more than was expected.

Darlene had the fastest overhand in Barlow history, everybody knew that. She said to Shazam, "Want to catch some?" Everybody except Shazam knew this was a test. Beautiful Hair held out her excellent glove to Shazam and Shazam took it, and she and Darlene walked away from one another out there, Darlene went almost to the lightning tree and threw the first one.

Shazam gets Beautiful Hair's glove under it perfect and she heaves it back to Darlene quick and hard. That was the first time I noticed her strong arms. We none of us girls had strong arms like that. Not even Darlene.

I remember so clear like a photograph the sight of those two throwing back and forth, Darlene in her fastness and Shazam in that tablecloth dress, not missing one single catch. Others came along, Manny and Lola and Lila. We all just stood and watched Shazam for her first time at Barlow, and I happened to look up into the school and there was Coach Rayfield standing in the window of his room, watching down too.

I think back to that day. *Thwop, thwop, thwop,* the ball landing in their gloves.

We didn't even know yet Shazam was both left and right handed.

And then the bell rang to go inside the school to begin sixth grade. I always love the fresh varnish smell of a new grade, and the different direction of the sun coming in the room, it's never the same as the year before that we have all got tired of. This year we went to Mrs. Winters's room, which has the bell rope just outside the door and we got to ring it in turns, being sixth graders and the oldest ones.

By afternoon the temperature was warmed up and we had our first official practice. Some boys agreed to be our opposing team and Shazam fielded very good against them with a ratty old glove from the sports box. When she got up to bat she slammed the ball way out to the lightning tree twice. And she ran good.

And wearing that awful dress. It was a mystery where she came from. Coach Rayfield went up to her after practice. "Shazam, you got a good swing. Shazam, you *aiming* those balls out there?"

Shazam she looks at him off-guard, and she says, "Yeah." Coach Rayfield looks at her mystified like the rest of us. He says he's real glad she came to Barlow this year.

Shazam told Coach she wanted to pitch. She just up and said it. We none of us would just say it like that, we would wait to be chose. He explained how we had Ila Mae as our pitcher already but we needed a relief pitcher too, and he said how Shazam had the gift of an outfielder.

"We really need you out there, you'll be real important to our team," says Coach Rayfield in his way that always made you want to play good for him.

Shazam looked at him with those eyes.

Coach Rayfield said in his serious face to all of us, "We got to beat them Ridgers this time. And you the gals that are gonna do it. We got high hopes, the whole darn town gonna be counting on all a you, so you go get it." Then he made us yell our spirit yell,

"Go, go, go!
Go, Barlow, go!
They did it back then, we can do it again!
Go, Barlow, go!"

Barlow won many of the games in history. Including the time Beautiful Hair's sister hit a home run in 1945, and many more games we do not remember on account of they were not in our lifetime.

Then Coach walked off the field with Manny. He said, "You went to church and prayed for a good outfielder to come and live here, Manny?" He was kidding Manny like always.

"No, I did not, Coach," Manny said. "I might of. But I didn't. I never even thought about no new outfielder coming here. So there."

Coach laughed. "Well, I did," he said in a low voice that some of us heard.

Somehow we got the idea God sent her right here to Barlow to win the Bat trophy back from the Ridge.

Audrey, catcher

I had been stacking cordwood to build my strength up. I stacked 4 cords at home and then me and Darlene stacked 4 more down behind the Flying Horse gas station where my great-uncle Beau works. Down there he has the big wooden board with all the Bat 6 scores on it from all the years. Actually it is a bunch of boards nailed to 2 posts, it is 16 foot high, and Uncle Beau has painted the scores on, he even did all the scores in history, back to 1899. Anybody driving up the road could see that board. He would always put Barlow wins in red and Ridge wins in green, he used a half-inch brush on the whitewashed boards. By the time our turn came, Barlow had 23 wins and the Ridge had 26. While me and Darlene stacked the cordwood, Uncle Beau kept teasing us about he would need to have the red paint can ready on May 28 so he could letter in BARLOW PIONEERS and our winning score.

For the first 5 days of our 6th grade, Coach Rayfield had us pull slips of paper out of his old umpire's hat he used to use during the war when the umps was all far away from home fighting for our country and he had to be one.

These slips of paper, which Darlene and Wink wrote the words on, said "first base" or "shortstop" or "pitcher" on them, all the different positions. And then whoever got that slip of paper had to play that position for the afternoon. Lola and Lila were included, naturally. Even though it looked like Lola was out of a job with Shazam suddenly amongst us.

The volunteer boys formed a batting lineup and we fielded. They sometimes hit very hard and especially Toby could hurt you when he slid into your base. Coach Rayfield told the boys they couldn't play if they were not going to be serious gentlemen in their playing. Of course they made "serious gentlemen" faces behind his back, but they played by the rules.

We fielded grounders and Coach Rayfield told us, "Descend slow, *with* the ball as it comes to you. You seen those airplanes in the movies. Do it the way them planes do. Slow, slow, slow. Don't just drop down when the ball gets there."

Beautiful Hair Hallie could even field grounders backhand very smooth, she was beginning to teach Manny and Lola and me the year before, but we none of us could do it like her. It was partly having her own glove and partly her God-given talent. And Coach Rayfield he says, "That's a good backhand there, but remember, Hallie, you might delay 2 seconds using backhand, you could give the runner 6 or 8 feet to the base." Some of the boys hit very hard grounders and they got real smarty when you let it get past you, so we was all trying very hard to field them good.

And we had to catch flies in the outfield. "Point your nose to that ball up there," Coach hollers. "Feet *wider* than shoulder width! Wider! And keep your eye on the ball. We got to get us some sun practice so you can learn to put that glove up there to hide the sun from your eyes."

And he did. He got us out from social studies on sunny days, and we practiced stepping over to the side and putting up our glove when the sun was in the outfield.

Well, Shazam hardly didn't need him to say those reminders even once. Not more than once anyway. She knew how to field like she knew how to hit.

Coach Rayfield yells to us, "*Mem*orize your base. You can't take your eyes off the ball to *find* your bag. Your foot's gotta *know* where that bag is."

The day Shazam drew the slip of paper with "pitcher" on it, she struck out Jimmy with the birthmark once and she also put 2 boys out at home by throwing to Beautiful Hair who was catcher that day. Kayo Riley and Jimmy with the birthmark on his next time up were those boys. They was both a little what you might call mad, but it was plain as the nose on their face they was out fair and square.

Then the boys switched onto the field and we got to be the batters. Beautiful Hair and Wink were our best hitters. Well, Ila Mae too. Darlene and me were our best long-ball hitters till Shazam come to Barlow. Shazam got one between center and right, and the boys couldn't agree on who would get it, so she went all the way to second base. Next time up, she got one right over the head of the shortstop. She said she knew he wouldn't be able to catch it. She got to third on that one because the boys in the outfield was talking and not paying attention.

At first the boys all wanted to be our volunteer opposing team, but they dwindled. They were mixed in their feelings about playing against girls. And, well, you could tell if you looked at them halfway straight they did not like a girl being so good like Shazam was.

There was a odd thing about Shazam's eyes. When it was people she was looking at, they shifted around. But when it was a ball, she kept her eyes on it with full concentration.

The whole first week of school we didn't hardly know much more about her than the first day, but then we started to know some, on account of Ila Mae asked and got a answer of very small information from her mom.

Shazam, center field

The fire dream come nobody can get out all fire all around.

Ila Mae, pitcher

I got home from the first day of 6th grade and changed into old clothes to do the chickenhouse chores and throw a ball at the fence. While I was changing into my slacks I told my mom about the odd new girl. Where's she live, my mom wants to know. I say she lives with her grandmother out by the gravel pit.

"No kidding?" my mom says. "I'm suprised that child is here. She's 11 years old already? Time flies, that's for sure."

But she didn't really explain me this girl.

"That would by Floy's girl. Poor little thing, Floy never did have good luck."

I ask her what she means.

She tells me it is not for my ears.

This made me want to know all the more.

I said to the other girls to go ask their moms, but no-body's mom told anything clear. They just said like my mom, That must by Floy's girl, poor little thing, she's 11 already? Like that. Brita Marie's mom said Shazam's mother needed to get on her feet and she must of sent Shazam here to live. She would not say no more about it.

Mrs. Winters, which was our teacher, was the only one wouldn't call her Shazam. She said, "I will call you Shirley and you will answer to your proper name. Shirley is a very pretty name."

Shazam give that look of hers to Mrs. Winters but she could not hold it. Her eyes shifted in a moment and you could feel her giving in. Mrs. Winters always called her her proper name and she answered to it. The whole time.

But to Coach Rayfield and the rest of us she was Shazam like she said she was. I think we thought calling her Shazam was okay if she would help us win that game of our lifes.

Shazam fastened onto Brita Marie, and Mrs. Winters told Brita Marie she should be Shirley's special friend for a while, till she could learn to mingle. Brita Marie went along with it, but it was too big of a job for 1 person.

Shazam needed study help, for she did not have school skills. There was a rule we had to be good enough of students to even set our foot on the ball field in the Bat. Without Shazam we would of had enough girls for a team, but the truth is, Lola would of been our 9th girl and she was not near the athletic sports talent of Shazam. Lola had been counting on getting to play a position, but she and her twin Lila had to accept their reality of being managers and general subs when Shazam come here.

Audrey was our good arithmetic star, she made Shazam learn the time tables, for the teachers in Shazam's childhood had not did so. Well, part of the time tables. Audrey got Shazam up to the 5's before giving up on the 6's and 7's. Shazam got real snarly when the problems got too hard and Audrey said no softball game in the universe was that important, she did not like getting blamed for arithmetic being hard to do. Wink took over and they got through the 9's, but they had to skip the 6's and 7's completely.

Shazam did not get snarly with Mrs. Winters. She just stopped doing her work partway down the page and sat in her desk staring. She would stare at the bulletin board where we had the map and papers of good schoolwork up there. Brita Marie and Jimmy with the birthmark always had something of theirs on the bulletin board, they were the smartest in 6th grade.

Shazam she didn't get it about normal things like not staring at Jimmy with the birthmark. She kept doing it till she got bored of it. Jimmy was so used to strangers being rude and staring, he pretended he didn't even notice. Brita Marie distracted Shazam when she did odd things like that. See what I mean about it was a lot of work to be Shazam's friend?

When the new geography books come in a truck, Shazam was the first to say she wanted to carry the boxes of them. Mrs. Winters let her do it and she praised her very nice for her strong arms and hard work. Shazam didn't hardly learn her geography, though.

She would of got all bad grades if it wasn't for the girls helping her study for the quizzes, like what all the 48 state capitals are. And I don't think she ever did get her long-division problems to come out right.

But she was such a natural-born athlete she was going to win that trophy bat back for us. The trophy was the bat that had the name of the winners and the Most Valuable Player carved in it for 5 years back. There was many trophy bats, some of them up on the Ridge, some of them here at Barlow, but the one up on the Ridge for 2 years was the one we wanted. Just over my shoulder all the time I heard Coach Rayfield saying, "Keep your arm good, Ila Mae. Pitching wins games."

The truth is I was working on my pitching for 2 years already. I never had took my mind from it. Even when everybody had snow shaking off their boots in the coatroom all winter long and they didn't have no thought to ball season I was thinking about pitching. Me and my brother A.J., we practiced out back. He taught me my windup and we practiced striking each other out. We would practice till my mom come out on the porch, stepping very careful so she wouldn't slip on the ice where the porch was tilty. One time the year before she yelled, "Ain't you doing anything else your whole lifes?" Steam puffed out her mouth.

You should see my brother A.J. laugh when she said that. He said back to her, "No. Me and Ila Mae is Christy Mathewson of the New York Giants. He pitched 373 winning games, ya know. He's in the Hall of Fame, ya know."

Then my oldest brother he said, "New York Giants, my foot. You ain't gone no more further than Portland."

My mom she said like always, "Don't you dare hit the cooler box," she meant the window box where we keep the milk and eggs in winter. And she went inside to continue being proud.

It was a credit to my brother A.J. I could pitch left and right both. He made me do it and I was so glad. He soaked his hands in pickle brine to keep them tough, so I did it also. I did not do it as often as him.

I had once long ago thought maybe I could even be Most Valuable Player for our year. That was conceited of me, but I confess it did enter into my mind. Because I just loved playing ball, it felt so good when it went good. Not just when I was striking people out. Not just that. It was even more fun when the other team would have maybe a runner on first and their next batter up hit a long drive into right field, and I'd go over between third and home because the runner might get to third or she might even try for home but if I was there to catch the throw I could get her out. I don't mean I wanted to take away the job of Darlene or Audrey on that play, but the truth is, you never know just how the throw will go.

And that's what kept my interest. Like some people like frogs or stamp collecting or something like that. I just loved playing ball.

Here is the bad thing that happened and I thought I understood it but I didn't. I should of caught on. It happened one morning before school and I promised God I would keep it a secret. I just didn't catch on. Then.

Even though it was cold and gray, me and Shazam was walking out to throw a ball around between the stump and the lightning tree, and Nob and Ruby Shimatsu's little boy went running past, wearing a red sweater, tagging after Toby whose mother brought them to school that day. Shazam she took a look at that little 1st grade boy and she said to me, "Hey, there's a Jap. Right in this school."

I told her we can't say that word at our school. And besides, I point out to her Billy Shimatsu is just a little boy. Only 6 years old, he couldn't hurt anybody even if he wanted to.

"Don't you remember Pearl Harbor?" Shazam says to me. She said it very patriotic, accusing me for not remembering Pearl Harbor, which I admit I did not remember all the time. It was something of our young childhood and it was all over and done with, thank the good Lord above.

"That was way back in the war," I reminded her. "There ain't a war on anymore, not for a long time."

"I don't want to go to school with Japs," she goes on like I didn't say anything.

I tell her Billy was born in the U.S.A. just like we were. I tell her Beautiful Hair's sister has baby-sat him before. He was just a little boy like others.

"Maybe I'll quit this school if they have Japs," she says.

I knew for a fact this was a cockeyed thing to say. Shazam was here with her grandmother for there wasn't a single nother place to go with her own mother not on her feet yet.

I said to her what about playing on our Bat 6 team, and her mouth gets sideways and lipped in.

I backed up about five steps and I toss her the ball and she tosses it back. We do that a few times, each time backing up a few more steps till I was almost at the blackberry tangle, and we toss the ball till the bell rings. I wanted Shazam to cool off about little Billy Shimatsu.

When the bell rang, we went slow toward the door, and I talked to her in a low voice. I tell her it's a rule of our life, we can't say that word she said, we'd get punished bad. And I tell her she's a great ball player. I tell her Coach would not let her play on the team if she said that word. And besides, God hears everything we say, and God don't like it when we say bad words.

Shazam looked at me with those mystery eyes and then she looked away, and I couldn't tell if she couldn't catch on, or if she didn't want to catch on, or if she caught on but wanted me to think she didn't catch on, or if she was a Martian come from Mars to Barlow by mistake. But her mouth did not look that dangerous way no more. We went inside to school.

I didn't tell nobody what Shazam said out there, so she could play in the Bat on May 28. God heard her, but I couldn't help that, it was already done.

Brita Marie's harmless uncle from the other war and Toby's idle relative that always sat on the Barlow Store porch with him, plus the gimpy-legged dog that sat alongside them, the whole lot of them moved inside even before the time of the World Series.

It looked like a cold winter ahead.

Shazam, center field

I try to remember those 7 times I keep seeing the fire dream my mom in that dress screaming the bombing. The 6 times too. Audrey says come on Shazam whats 7 X 8 I can't remember how to do it there is those bad bombers. Whats 7 X 6 Shazam them bad people bombing the harbor.

Shadean, Daisy, and Vernell

Shadean, pitcher

y mom and dad started taking me to the Bat 6 game when I was in diapers.

I said to myself at the very beginning of 6th grade, This might be the best year of my life. We live near the school and I had watched the big girls having their practices after school for many years. I had wanted to pitch our Bat 6 as long as my memory goes back to. And now I was getting to. Tootie and me had very good signals, we quizzed them to each other in notes in school and Mrs. Porter didn't catch us.

The Bat tradition is such an old one. Way back in the 1800s some pioneers came on the Oregon Trail and the first place they settled was down at the Barlow area. But things didn't run smooth among the men, they disagreed about the road, then they disagreed about the sewer, then they disagreed about the church, and there was too much arguing all around. So one group picked up with their families and moved farther up the creek till they ended up here on the Ridge. And then one of the McHenry boys shot a bear right on the ridge, so they named it that. You can still see the bearskin hanging on the wall in the back of McHenrys' Store, right above the desk, beside the pictures of all the McHenrys that have run the store and fought in both wars. So we live on Bear Creek Ridge, 14 and ⅔ miles up the creek from the first town which is Barlow, named after the Barlow Road, and that was named after Sam Barlow, a pioneer.

And the men of the different towns went on not talking to each other. They didn't even ride their horses down there to trade or anything.

So the ladies decided enough was enough, they wanted peace between the 2 towns. After a bad winter they arranged a ball game in the spring. They agreed to use alder branches and a leather ball, and the ladies made teams to play against each other all in good fun. They thought, Well, the men can't watch us playing our game for a whole afternoon and not say *anything* to one another, can they? And they arranged to take along baskets of food too. See, they were forcing the men to have a social.

Guess what, they were right. That was in May of the year 1899. Not all at once in that same afternoon, but slowly the men began being friendly. By having their game all the ladies caused peace to break out.

Doesn't that show something?

And one of the original ladies is still around. She played in that first game, her name is old Louella. She's as you might say a hero for being so old and having her tragedies and coming to the game every year. She is very wrinkly. A brownish photograph of her in her old ballgame dress is in the trophy case. She was a Bear Creek Ridge girl but then she married a Barlow boy so she is an honor to both places. Then her husband died in the first war and her son died in the second one. Every year she comes to the game and sits in her rocking chair they bring along for her. She always cheers for both teams.

So ever since then the girls of Barlow and the girls of the Ridge played a game in the spring. In the beginning it was girls and women, whoever wanted to play. Then it became only 6th grade girls because that was all the farther their schools went up to in those olden days.

And in those old times they didn't have rules like ours. Not even regulation bats or anything modern.

Even though the Ridge farmers got richer than the Barlow ones because of the better soil and less frost and closer water, the 2 towns stayed friendly in playing the game. There was hardly any bad feelings left by the time we got to 6th grade.

I didn't know I was going to end up telling the whole historical story. I didn't mean to tell more than my share.

By the time the big dogwood at the schoolhouse door had no leaves left, we knew we had to have more bats and balls, so we had a bake sale outside the Grange Hall on Election Day, and I was in charge of the money. We earned $13.00, enough to buy three Spalding softballs, as well as three Wilson Champ bats. The big surprise was that Truman beat Dewey and he is our President again. My parents were happy but some were not.

Mrs. Porter said I had to keep my mind on one thing mainly: to pitch more strikes than balls. This might seem too obvious. But it's so important. My dad and me painted a strike zone target in the barn, and I practiced pitching to the corners of it.

Tootie and I had worked and worked on this. Even the summer before. We'd go over to the school and pitch and catch for anyone who would join in. Sometimes we would find someone just hanging around McHenrys' Store porch and they'd come over and try to hit my pitches. Grownups even. One day the minister from over at the church was at the store and Tootie just up and said to him did he want to come across the road and play with us. He put down the shoelaces he was buying and came with her. He helped chase some of the foul balls he hit, and once I struck him out with inside pitches. Then he went back to finish his grocery shopping.

It was the very same summer Tootie discovered Aki and we got her on our team.

Mr. Porter, our handsome assistant coach, told me I had good pitcher's stuff. I said what did he mean and he said I concentrated quite good and I had different pitches, not all the same kind, and I had good endurance. In practices he kept wanting to have a runner — any runner — on third so as to make me pitch in all that nervousness. I did pretty good, too.

And there was base stealing. We practiced over and over, second, third, and home plate, throwing to catch a base stealer. I think maybe we practiced this more than anything. Daisy and Kate and Tootie even begged people to come and practice with us. "You can steal bases so we get the practice." They got some people to do it, Jerry McHenry and Piper and Darrell and Donald in our grade, but they lost interest quite easy and we had to bribe them with doing their lunch-table duties. Tootie and Kate and Daisy did not mind doing that.

But Kate couldn't come to practice on Tuesdays because that was her day to milk the cow. It was her father's strict rule every child in their family had to milk one day. And in Kate's only year to play the Bat, too.

And Lorelei and Aki both had to miss practices because their fathers needed them in the orchard. Aki even got permission to miss whole days of school. Their orchard, being in so terrible condition from not being sprayed proper when the McHenrys were taking care of it and they couldn't do everything at the same time, had poor little fruit and besides that, Aki's father couldn't afford to pay a lot of pickers. Her big brother Shig had to stay out of high school till the harvest was over. He only went to school on Mondays till the middle of October. The Mikamis had to sell their tractor when they went away, and Shig drove the McHenrys' tractor that they were lending to them, up and down the orchard rows to pick up the full boxes of fruit and load them on the wagon to carry them to the truck that was the McHenrys' also. Then one of the McHenry brothers drove the truck loaded with boxes of fruit to the packing house.

Aki's brother is so smart he doesn't really need to go to school, I heard one of the teachers say at church, he could get his lessons in 2 seconds flat. It was just something I overheard.

And then there was chicken pox. Daisy was the first one to get them. She must have brought them up from the Catholics down in River Bend where she goes to church. But Susannah probably brought them up here too, from her music lessons down there.

It went right through the school.

But we continued having our indoor drills after school anyway. And when it wasn't raining, we had our practice games with whatever boys would play.

The weather got wintery and nasty. We had early snow. Meaning I had to practice in the barn with the target on the wall. And my dad was so fussy about his shiny new John

Deere tractor that was parked in there, I didn't dare put a dent in it anywhere. He even polished that tractor, he was so in love with it.

And then after the first snow we had bare roads for days and days. Mr. Porter went out running with us to strengthen our legs. "We don't want to play the Bat with our tired winter legs, do we?" he said. The truth is that running along with Mr. Porter was fun, he is so handsome. Even with his arm partly gone from being in the war.

Well, my mom and dad came back from the parents' Bat 6 meeting all sad about how the farmers down there in Barlow got too much of their fruit frozen and how raggedy poor some of them are. Still, those parents did their part in volunteering for parent committees and voting on everything. It is just hard luck on them about the trees down there in the frost pocket.

But we heard they had good luck too. They had a new girl that was a phenomenon. She came in on a Greyhound bus in time to go to 6th grade down at Barlow and she could hit anything, she could field anything. That's what the people at the meeting told. They said she lived with her grandmother out by the gravel pit and because of this girl they were likely to take home the trophy that had been up here on the Ridge for 2 years.

Well, we had our new girl too, but she was not actually new, she was back. Aki was so good to have, she was fun and she did her schoolwork excellent and she was super good at first base. And she was a hitter, too. Like Tootie said about Aki's playing, "Hubba hubba ding ding."

I felt in my bones we were to have a great Bat 6. I felt it might turn out to be the best year of my life.

I heard their pitcher down there at Barlow soaked her hands in pickle brine. I never heard of such a thing. I said to myself I wouldn't do that for anything.

Daisy, third base

My name is Daisy. It never has been anything else.

I hate being called Loose Lips, it was not anything I even understood way back then in 1st grade when Herby shouted out, and some of them called me that bad name ever since. No true friend would ever call me that. Nobody but Lorelei knew how many times I cried over it.

Me and Lorelei got to be partners for the social studies countries, we chose Italy for it has many beautiful sculptures there. And gondolas, we would adore to ride in one and fall in love with the rowers. They sing songs.

Lorelei's father has scads of books on shelfs. Two of them are Italy books full of holy paintings and naked statues. So we went on the school bus to her house to study our report and her mother had such a good supper of chops from their sheep and mint jelly from their mint and apples. I ate so much my belly ached. Then when my dad came to their house to take me home, he would not even go inside their house because of Lorelei's father. He sat in the driveway and honked the horn. He wouldn't give an inch.

I was so mad.

My dad was in the war, I already told about that bad name I got called. That whole time my mom had us alone and he could get killed any moment. We did so many prayers for his life to be saved in the war and it came true, he came home all together, not torn apart like some men did.

Well, Lorelei's father he does not believe in no war so he had to go to a camp for those kind of people when wartime come. And my father said no man that wouldn't fight for his country is a friend of his. He said you might as well be a traitor to your country if you wouldn't do your manly duty overseas.

Me and Lorelei were friends anyway, and I was so embarrassed about my dad.

But my dad is so precious to me due to him being away for that long time. And I wanted to play extra good on May 28 for my father to see. I knew he wanted to be proud of me that day for all time to come.

And for one other reason too I wanted to play extra good. I was thinking if our team would win, and everybody would be cheering and jumping up and down and hugging each other, everybody would be joyful and friendly even to those they didn't know good.

Well, my dad would get so happy and proud he would

just all of a sudden be cheering and Lorelei's dad would be cheering too, and my dad would accidentally speak to Lorelei's dad, and the bad feelings would be gone, poof. Deep in my heart I wished this would happen.

It would be like before, back in 1899, when they played the first Bat game of all. The men started speaking to each other and let their grudges go.

Lorelei and me were both different, due to her father and my religion that is Catholic, we go to church down at St. Mary's way down at River Bend. I probably gave Lorelei the chicken pox. But then others got it too. It could of come with me from St. Mary's where some kids had it, or it could of come with Susannah on her music-lesson day down there. I think I gave it to Vernell too because I shared my sandwich with her before I knew I had the pox. And she shared her chocolate milk with me like always. Poor Vernell, her mind has always wandered and then she got chicken pox and had to miss school when we learned how to multiply fractions and she was so mixed up about arithmetic anyway.

I was almost sure we could win that game. I was glad to be playing third base, we practiced over and over again the drill of Daisy to Kate to Aki. If a Barlow hitter came to bat with a runner on first, if she hit in my territory I'd field it and send it to Kate as fast as I could, she'd put the runner out at second and then send it to Aki and Aki would put the runner out at first.

How great it would be if we won because of something I did.

My father would be so thrilled. So thrilled.

He didn't even know my mom traded Lorelei's mom her ginger pear honey recipe for their chili recipe. He had been eating the chili of Lorelei's family for 2 years and he didn't know it. His own wife too. It just goes to show you, his resenting grudge was all in his mind.

If the ball would come in my territory with the bases loaded and no outs. Daisy to Kate to Aki. It was so exciting to expect in the future.

Mr. Porter was strict about everybody had to move on every pitch. "Nobody just stands there. Keep those Barlow players worried, keep our confidence up. They see us moving around, they know we mean business out there." Well, I remembered. I remembered every time.

And Mr. Porter said, too, "When we play our game well, it makes Barlow play well. It makes things better for everybody, that's sportsmanship."

And that was odd, on account of I thought we were supposed to play good so they would play bad.

I would keep my mind all on my own business but except what my cousin over at the Consolidated High did with his buddies and us girls thought it was so funny and the grownups did not. Four boys including my cousin went and painted a bright green stripe down the middle of the highway right through town, green and white being the Bear Creek Ridge Mountaineer colors on account of the forest trees and the mountain snow. The boys did it way back on Halloween but they were still doing their Community Service on into the winter. Their Community Service was the job of filling in all the pavement holes from one end of town to the other, and they had to remove the green stripe besides. It was the Community Council made them do it. They try to make fair play out of things that started out unfair.

Those boys had to work on Saturdays and all the cars had to steer around them. Many people hollered out the car windows at them how they shouldn't of done what they did.

Vernell, manager and general sub

Aki helped me with reading, her desk was behind mine. Mrs. Porter said it was all right, I would just turn around and point to the word and Aki would tell me.

And also I thought I was lucky Aki came to live here, I would of had to play if she didn't live here. I didn't really want to play in the Bat game and not catch the ball good in front of everybody. It was bad enough at practices with just the girls. I thought it would be worst in front of many people. I spent the winter hoping they would not need any subbing, I wanted to be manager but not have to play.

Mr. Porter just said Oh come on Vernell we all want to have a good team and a good time. I was too shy to tell him

I wished they would do it without me, I just wanted to do manager duties. I could easy keep the bats in a line and make sure the water can didn't spill. I watched how they did it the year before, it looked like fun. Much funner than missing the ball on the ball field and having people say Oh look how Vernell missed the ball.

In fact from 5th grade I prayed not to have to play in the game in our year. And then Aki came, the answer to my prayer.

Staying home with chicken pox was not so bad but I missed the girls. Daisy always shared her lunch with everybody and I wondered what the school lunch was each day too. I did not miss the indoor drills we had to do, it was hard to remember what each drill was, there were too many.

Having the chicken pox down in the swale where we live it was lonely with only just trees and swamp. But the heron that lives close by was fun to watch out the window, and my mom got me a Captain Marvel comic and a Wonder Woman too.

And old Louella which lives near us was over and my mom was giving her a home perm on her old thin hair. My mom put the towel around her shoulders where she was setting in the chair, front of the sink, and old Louella said, "Now, Vernell, you gals got a real important privilege to play the Bat this year."

I just stood there. I would not want to tell old Louella I did not really want to play the game.

"Good sportsmanship, that is life, don't you forget it, gal."

I just stood there again.

"You hear me, gal? Vernell, you hear me? What'd I say?"

I told her, "You said Good sportsmanship that is life don't you forget it."

My mom looked at me and made with her eyes like it was OK for me to go read my Wonder Woman now.

Darlene, Shazam, Beautiful Hair Hallie, and Alva

Darlene, third base

In the first big snow we had a project to help the little kids of 2nd grade make their snowmen and the next day their eyes and buttons was gone and there was raccoon tracks in the snow. The cats' water froze on the porch and we had a whole box of pears nibbled into by possums, you could see their eyes in the night. My dad being the snowplow driver one morning real early he seen 3 deer come down out of the woods to eat. Over at Ila Mae's they had deer in their yard even.

Some days there wasn't any sunset, the daylight just slid away gray.

But then there was sunny days too at times and Coach would send us out running to condition our bodies and get endurance. He did not run with us on account of he is getting along in years. One sunny day he said we had to run up past the goat lady's house, but Ila Mae didn't want to. We all thought it was because it's haunted. We told her she was just being superstitious, people been going past it for years with no damage done. The haunt was all inside the house, it couldn't get ahold of you just running along, not if you ran fast.

The goat lady was so old she was almost not real anymore she was so paper-thin, and all she did was yell at you, "You all get outa my garden!" It wasn't even any kind of garden anymore but some cabbages and old weeds laying in the mud and snow. It really was not a dangerous place.

But we found out it was a different reason why Ila Mae did not want to go anywhere near it. When we ran past, six boys from the high school was there, hammering and measuring and putting new boards in the goat lady's porch which was all broke down. Ila Mae's oldest brother was there amongst them and Ila Mae didn't want us to know about it.

The truth made her embarrassed so bad. On Halloween night them boys had lifted up an outhouse from somebody's orchard and hoisted it up on a Ford pickup of one of their dads. In the middle of the night they hauled it all the way up the highway to the Consolidated High School and they unloaded it right smack onto the principal's parking place exactly in front of the flagpole.

So the Community Council made them do part of their Community Service work putting new boards in the sagging porch of the goat lady's shack, and the rest of their hours they had to weed and rake and prune in the Valley View Cemetery. That cemetery was there since 1901.

When it got explained to us, we told Ila Mae it was not her fault her brother done that prank, the shame was his, not hers. And besides, you could look at it as a good thing them boys done, so the cemetery could get some self-respect back. There was dead loved ones laying there amongst overgrown vines and trees till those boys did that scandal with the privy. For years that cemetery was not kept up neat and it was a disgrace, everybody knew that.

Those boys were not allowed to go into the Barlow Store or McHenrys' Store either one, not till they got the cemetery looking proud. They were also not allowed in church, either the Barlow Gospel or the church up on the Ridge, wherever their families belonged. They couldn't get their privileges back till they got their hours done.

We explained and explained Ila Mae didn't need to feel shame for her whole family. We went running on up the hill, and Alva pointed out how good it was the poor old goat lady wouldn't be falling through them rotten boards on her way to feed her goats.

I wish I'd of seen the principal's face when he drove his car to school and saw the privy in the middle of his parking place. I bet he had a fit.

And Wink was sick with chicken pox and she couldn't do the endurance running that day.

The next person with the chicken pox was Manny who

got her red bumps on the bus before school and had to go right back home again when the driver took the bus back.

Many of the 3rd grade had chicken pox, and part of all other grades too.

I got to thinking. Before this new Shazam come here, we was all mostly regular. We was different heighths, Wink being such a tall giant and the rest of us very average. And there was no real fat ones, unless you counted me, which is on the beefy side.

Audrey was one of the 2 arithmetic champions. The other one was a boy, Toby. And there was Kayo Riley, he was average in most things except niceness, he was above average in niceness. He would often hit fungoes to we girls when the other boys merely wanted to play war in their fort behind the blackberry tangle.

Beautiful Hair Hallie of course had the most beautiful hair. Anybody could tell you that. And she was a base stealer. She was also our best hitter till Shazam came, and her sister was MVP in 1945.

Brita Marie was the smartest one in everything but arithmetic, with Jimmy with the birthmark tying with her for best grades. Brita Marie's folks have the Barlow General Store. But she is not spoilt, she does not have candy and Popsicles no more often than us. Her mom gives our class a new supply of crayons from the store every single year.

And then there was Lola and Lila that got sulky sometimes, thinking one of them was getting treated unfair. But they was both nice girls, their dad fixed the frozen plumbing at the school in the wintertime when we was in 4th grade and he never charged the school one red cent for his pains.

And there was Ila Mae with her hoodlum brother and her nice one.

And then there was me, I do not have no bedroom of my own, I would hear the girls griping of cleaning their rooms but I do not have one to clean. I would clean it very good. If it wasn't just the corner of the living room on the foldout. My mom said we could build on someday but not yet.

My mom cleans house for the Doc up on the Ridge which has a daughter Susannah my age, her mother is the nurse. We played together a few times when I had to go with my mom or when they brought my mom home. Susannah has her own room and a pond out back besides. Susannah and me caught six frogs there one time the summer after 4th grade. They have a piano and also they have Popsicles in their freezer compartment of their fridge. I confess I envied that.

Maybe I was the poorest one. But Audrey lived in a poor house too, with her back porch held up by stacks of bricks and their dishes for supper all chipped with no milk glasses matching each other.

But I had a specialness. Coach Rayfield himself told me I had the best overhand in Barlow history. I would not brag on it, but it was a fact. It was because of my overhand Coach told me in 5th grade to shape up my studies, he had talked to the teacher and they was looking over the grades of the girls for his 1949 Pioneer team, and they was worried about me. I told him I would study hard and it was the truth. Because there was times that a girl did not get to play due to her bad grades, there was one in 1947, she did not get to be on the team on account of she didn't pay attention to her school-work and make her social-studies reports.

After Coach talked to me, I paid attention very hard and I got all the capital letters very straight on the line, and I got my time tables pretty good. Mrs. Winters said how she was happy I was listening so good, I got both the North and South Dakota capitals before anybody in one of our State Quiz Games on a day when Brita Marie was home with chicken pox.

In despite of our differences, we girls was all regular. That's the point.

Well, we was different religions, most of us going to the Gospel Church, with the real name of Assembly of Disciples' Gospel Church. But the twins of Lola and Lila belonged to the Mormons and Latter-Day Saints down to River Bend, along with Kayo Riley and some Ridge kids. They said they were not saints, it is just a church name. And Jimmy with the birthmark was a Catholic, they had to go all the way to River Bend to church too.

Well, that word religion brings up Manzanita, our left field.

I'm not saying she was peculiar in the head. Nothing

queer about Manny. Except one thing and it was God. She got the spirit down to the tent revival in River Bend when we was 9. Or maybe 8. No, I'm sure we was 9. She was talking in tongues and we none of us felt right about it.

Many grownups got the spirit that day, with the music and the good preaching, but no other little children, she was the only one.

It was more like she got the heebie-jeebies than the spirit. But she insisted to believe it was really God in her heart.

Manny was never a fanatical or anything. She just got the spirit that time. She was still normal and regular to the naked eye.

But it was hard to know could we trust her judgment 100 percentage on the ball field. She might get the spirit with a fly heading straight for her, and lose the game for Barlow. There wasn't much chance of it. But still.

See how regular we all was? Very regular.

Then Shazam come to Barlow with her sports talent and her quick reflexes and her bad arithmetic and reading. And her poor old grandmother in her tumbledown house out there by the gravel pit. And those dresses somebody must of homemade for her. The lavender one she wore on Tuesdays and Thursdays was probably the worst, it was from a bedspread I would bet anybody. And her mother that hadn't got up on her feet yet. And this Shazam that had the real name of Shirley was the best sports athlete we ever saw.

It was in friendliness we pitched in to help Shazam. Brita

Marie even took her to the Gospel Church one time and you should of seen her not knowing when to stand up and sit down and she asked how come we say Amen, what does it mean, and all of us Christian girls not a single one amongst us could tell her what Amen is for.

When Brita Marie told her there was a Christmas play about the baby Jesus getting born, she wanted to be in it. We girls was all being in it so we said Come on, it will be fun. Well, not Lola and Lila, for their church is different. But all the rest of us.

That is how much we helped Shazam try to get regular.

Now that's enough about Shazam.

My main thing to remember in that whole winter of snow and mud and almost no outdoor practice was the long throw. Coach he says, "The long throw over to first, that could win us the game, Darlene. You keep that in mind. And study your studies so you can be on that field with us next May. How much is eight times nine?"

I tell him 72 and he says Good for you Darlene.

When the parents of everybody on both teams had their first meeting, Brita Marie's uncle got chose to be base umpire. The plate ump was a man from up on the Ridge, a dad of a boy. They aren't allowed to be dads of the team girls on account of they could be favored.

Shazam, center field

Them puka shells my dad give me. Pretty shells all on the necklace string I had them these many years. I look at them in the night with the flashlight. When the fire dream come I cant go back to sleep I look at them.

Hallie, right field

I kept my ball wrapped in my glove and I tied it up tight with twine when I wasn't using it. To get the glove shaped into a basket to always hold the ball right. My glove was a J.C. Higgins, personally endorsed by Bob Feller for all fielding positions, Bob Feller was in the World Series right then at the same time I got it from the catalogue with cherry picking money, $5.65 which I earned in 2 days in the summertime.

And it was my glove that made Shazam start to come close to me at first.

But it wasn't only just the glove or Shazam, it was partly me, too. That wrong dress she had on that first day that somebody had worked so hard to sew, planning the buttons to go all down the dress in a row. And those boy's shoes she was wearing was all spit-and-polished so shiny. I wanted to like her for that.

And also after the first couple of days she always called me Hallie. She began by calling me Beautiful Hair when she heard that name, but when I said would she call me Hallie in trade for me calling her Shazam like she wanted, she did it.

Coach Rayfield and his wife had us up to their house for weenies and Kool-Aid and announced the team, and Mrs. Rayfield had gone and baked a big apple spice sheet cake with a softball diamond on the green and brown frosting. She had decorated it with frosting drawings of all of us in our positions and our names over our heads like holy halos. There was Ila Mae, pitcher, Audrey, catcher. At first base there was big tall Wink, then Brita Marie at second, Alva our shortstop, and Darlene at third. In the outfield Mrs. Rayfield had put green grass and the three of us, Shazam at center, between Manny at left and me at right.

And that left out Lola and Lila from the starting players. We knew Lila couldn't catch or hit worth a darn, but Lola was pretty good and she was counting on being something more than a manager and general sub, which is where she ended up. Mrs. Rayfield had put Lola and Lila as managers over at our team's bench on the side of the cake.

That cake was the first we heard for sure about Lola. We felt bad for her, but we wanted to win that game.

When Coach announced the team, he made special care to announce them. "We'll be rich with two managers, right, gals? And they're our important sub players, too. Let's hear a cheer for our managers and subs, Lola and Lila, the swell job they're gonna do."

We cheered, "Yea, Lola! Yea, Lila! Yea, yea, Lola and

Lila!" They were really happy. But a cheer is only a cheer. It is only loud words. It wouldn't make me feel any better if I was Lola.

Then Coach said, "And my Dotty she'll come up to be our first-base coach," and we all got respectful in respect of Coach's hero daughter down at the state college. Everybody knew her name was on the bat in the trophy case for being MVP of 1940.

Coach Rayfield knew by heart who had won all the Bat games from the year 1899 and he recited them to us up at his house that day. He even remembered what years there wasn't enough girls to make a team and they played as best as they could anyway. The total was the Ridge had won 26 games and Barlow had won 23. "But Barlow has more assists *and* more double plays if you look at the record overall," says Coach. "You all know what that means?" He looks around at us all, scattered about his front room with plates of cake on our laps.

"It means we got *team*work down the hill here in Barlow, that's what it means. It means we ain't merely nine girls standing on a field watchin' the sun move across the sky and puttin' our gloves to the ground every now and then. It means —" He looks hard around the room. "It means every player on the field helps her team, because the team ain't nothin' without the cooperation of all a you. You hear that?"

Coach felt like a friend to all of us, standing there by the woodstove, all wound up with his pep. We all of us nodded our heads and said we heard it. Then we cheered 3 cheers for the Barlow Pioneers. And Mrs. Rayfield went into the bedroom and come out with 11 brand-new Wilson softball caps in bright red with a big white B on them, and she passed them around.

What a wonderful feeling it was, modeling our caps in Coach's front room, all looking at each other and saying how good they fit and how we would take good care of them till next May 28.

We gave 3 cheers for Mrs. Rayfield for such a good time at her house.

Shazam came over to sit beside me when it was time for seconds on cake. She says, "Your piece and my piece is neighbors on the cake, huh."

I said, "Yeah, they sure are neighbors. The outfield is our neighborhood," I made a joke. "Manny and me and you," I said.

"We can be in cahoots," says Shazam, serious and secret.

And she scoots over close to me on the bench. Anybody could see she was lonely. She didn't have a complete home like the rest of us, only her grandmother.

She says, "I can come to your place to practice." I look at her and she says, "We can trade off using your glove." I sat there not wanting to be rude and Shazam says, "I can come anytime, my grammama don't care."

Well, the whole first snow melted and the ground stayed hard, and my mom got it arranged so Shazam could come on a day Coach Rayfield had to go to a meeting of all teachers and we did not have team practice. I arranged to bring home a fielder's glove from the sports box so we would each have one. My mom sent a note to school on Monday that Shazam should take home to tell her grandmother she was invited for Wednesday, and the sun was shining that day on the cold ground. Even in November.

When we got to my house, my mom was beating up batter for ginger cookies. She said my dad would hit fungoes to us when he got home, so we went out past the woodshed to throw till he come home. I told Shazam about my dad's hearing, which is only half, ever since the war when he was at Iwo Jima. You can even yell on his right side and he hardly hears you. I had to tell her so she would talk to his left side.

She said, "The Japs got him over there."

Even though she said that bad word, I said Well, that was true, but it wasn't like they killed him. He's still alive, he's still my dad, he just can't hear as clear as normal people.

She said again, "The Japs got him." I decided she'd see when he got home that it wasn't so bad.

I said to her, "We can't say that word you said. Not since the war."

She said, "Well, they got him, didn't they?"

I said yes but we still can't say that word.

She said, "Let's play ball." We backed off and began to throw and catch.

When my dad got his G.I. Bill he went down to the state

college and he studied some courses on business. I mention this because of it made 2 differences. 1, he used to be only a sawyer at the mill. But after he studied on the G.I. Bill, he come back and they hiked him up to foreman and assistant boss of part of the mill due to his education he got down at the college. And we got our furnace fixed and a bigger hot water heater and other things besides. Because he made more money. By the time Shazam come over that day we'd had a refrigerator for 2 years, it was even hard to remember the old icebox. 2, my dad he felt so bad being away from us, first in the war and then down there at the college, he always played with us now as a lot of dads do not.

I did not mention these things to Shazam due to her not having a real home like me, I did not want to make her feel bad. With Shazam you never knew if she would be lurchy or steady about things. Instead I showed her the place where we seen the bear tracks last winter at the edge there, out where the fir trees begin.

She did not believe me at first but then I promised I would show her the plaster cast we made of that footprint. That bear paw print was in the front room right beside the radio.

We threw back and forth for a while, we could see our breaths in the air. Shazam could throw and catch for hours if you wanted her to.

When my mom had the ginger cookies out of the oven she hollered out to us to come get some. While we were in the house, Shazam wanted to see my room and I showed her. She saw my bedspread my mom made with the red and blue rickrack stripes on it and the bedside table my dad made for me. She saw on my wall the photograph of me and my sister at the beach and the scenic calendar we got from the Flying Horse gas station. And the curtains at the window matching the bedspread, I hemmed those after my mom sewed them.

Shazam she stands in the middle of my bedroom and says, "My father is long gone at the bottom of the sea, you'll never see him alive."

"Pardon me?" I said, with this sudden information.

"That's the whole truth," she said, solemn in her face.

We none of us girls knew this. I guess she told me first due to me having her over to my house.

"That's too bad," I said. I did not know what else to say.

"The Japs sent him to the bottom of the sea at Pearl Harbor, he'll never come back. You don't know how that is." Her mouth went a tight sideways way I only saw a couple of times before.

She was right. I didn't know how it was. I tried to say comforting words. "Your dad would be proud of how you play ball," I told her. I was catching on to no wonder she was stunted like. In her way of going along.

"That was December 7, 1941, I was just little, I never seen my father again this whole time since."

I told her again how he'd be proud. "He'd be proud of

your good sports talent," I said. I was starting to feel guilty having a father.

"He is still at the bottom of Pearl Harbor in that ship *Arizona*. The Japs bombed it without no warning, they went and killed all them dead soldiers fighting for our freedom."

That word. I already told her we couldn't say it. It was so long ago, and good Christians are supposed to forgive and forget. But it was not my dad that was at the bottom of a harbor leaving me to grow up wacky.

"The whole Navy tried to save him, them Japs made my mom a widow." She closed her arms around her stomach tight and got that look of a frying pan on her face.

I just stood there making a sympathy face, for I didn't know what to do.

"I'd still have my father like you do. My mom she ain't had time to get on her feet yet. The Japs took him away just like that." She kept her arms tight around herself. I stood there in my pretty bedroom feeling so sorry for this queer peculiar girl. It was 7 years and she was still so mad.

We heard the pickup come rattling up the driveway with my dad coming home from down at the mill, and we went out there. My dad said hi to Shazam and she said hi back. He brought out the bat and our other 2 softballs, one of them was coming unstitched.

I didn't know how Shazam would be with my dad, her being so concentrated on not having her own just 3 minutes ago. But she took to him right off. She hopped along beside him all the way out to the field.

We backed way off close to the woods. My dad he kept hitting the ball between us so we could practice knowing which ones was for center field and which was for right, and we practiced calling Mine when we went for it.

I was so glad I invited Shazam over to catch flies. Even though I just found out about her dead father. I never saw her so happy before as I saw her out there in the field with me and my dad. The Utsumis' cow was clinking her cowbell over in the pasture, and the sky was clear glassy blue.

Once when my dad turned around to chase the unstitched ball where it went crooked, Shazam hollers "Slugger!" to him and he didn't hear her. She repeats "Slugger!" again and he still did not hear. She was trying to be buddies. It looked like she needed a buddy so bad.

After we caught fungoes for a while, it was nearly dark. Shazam could borrow my bike to go home and ride it to school the next day, but my dad would not let her. It was more than four miles out to the gravel pit. He said, "Nothing doing. It'll get dark before you get up that road, you could get hit by a car. You get your coat while I start the pickup." Shazam did not have a coat but she picked up the old sweater she had laid down on the porch.

My mom come out on the porch and said to Shazam how nice it was she could come over to play. She handed Shazam a paper sack of ginger cookies. "You take these to your grandma, Shirley. You tell her I said hello."

Shazam took the sack of cookies and she said to my mom, "I could catch better if I had my own glove." My mom made no look on her face about Shazam not even saying thanks for the cookies.

"Sure you could, honey" was all she said. Shazam got in the pickup with my dad.

Old Mr. Utsumi was coming across the pasture with my dad's hayfork in his hand, he had fixed it for him by putting a new handle into the metal shaft, same as he had done with 2 shovels. He was walking his old limping walk he's had ever since his ankle was broke that time in the icy winter, and he was carrying his tall walking stick in his other hand.

My dad waved to Mr. Utsumi from the window of the pickup, and my mom told Shazam she hoped she could have a glove of her own by spring. My mom handed me a sack of cookies for Mr. Utsumi to take back across the pasture to his old wife Mrs. Utsumi, and Shazam and my dad they went rumbling out of the driveway. When Mr. Utsumi gave me the repaired hayfork I gave him the cookies and he said thank you and limped off across the pasture, lifting his walking stick up and down.

Partway across the pasture he turned around and waved. He had a cookie in his hand. The sun was on his old wrinkled face, and I thought how it was good he didn't hear Shazam say that bad word.

That was shocking news about Shazam's father. I asked my mom if she knew before. "Yes," she said. And she went on fixing supper. "How come you never said?" I said to her. She pointed me to the fork and knife drawer and said I should set the table. "I don't want to talk about war tragedies," she said, and I set the table. Everybody had war tragedies, and I agreed with my mom, I did not want to talk about them either. And her with her own husband deaf on one side.

But still. Your very own father. Absolutely dead forever.

My dad he said Shazam sure was a strange one, he kind of shrugged his shoulders about her. Well, not kind of. Really shrugged. He shook his head how sad it was for her getting moved around so many times in her life with her mother that wasn't on her feet yet. "But she has her grandmother out there by the gravel pit takes good care of her, she come out to the pickup to say thanks for bringing Shirley home safe."

Then he shrugged his shoulders again.

Well, I had done my good deed of having her over after school. And of course I called the girls that night and said about her dead father in Pearl Harbor and we some of us agreed on how tragedy could make a person loony. Not everybody thought that way. Audrey said, "Listen, crumptillions of children had fathers die in the war and they're normal people in despite of it." Audrey had a point.

I did not mention over the phone that word Shazam said. You would not say that word on the party line, there might be others listening in, or maybe even old Mr. or Mrs. Utsumi might be picking up the phone to make a call. You never know.

And even off the phone I decided I would not tell anybody. I was grown up enough to keep that bad secret. And I had told Shazam she couldn't say it anymore. I had done my part.

But thanks to God she didn't say it where our neighbors would hear. Old Mr. and Mrs. Utsumi. They even had to go away to a camp for the whole war just for being Japanese. And besides that, their son lost his life fighting in Italy on *our* side, the Germans killed him. His name is on the brass memorial over by the school. The whole war just broke old Mr. Utsumi's spirit, in my dad's opinion. Old Mr. Utsumi didn't hardly take much interest in anything when they came back. Old Mrs. Utsumi does her gardening, we can see her all bent over among her flowers and vegetables over there acrost the pasture.

Poor old soul. My mom makes my sister or me go over and check on the Utsumis every single cold day in the winter because of that time 2 years before when we didn't know for 3 days Mr. Utsumi had broke his ankle falling on the ice trying to get to the barn. It was only when my mom noticed no smoke coming up their chimney and she sent my sister over to find out. Well, old Mr. Utsumi was propped up on the bed and the fire was out. Their woodpile was froze and old Mrs. Utsumi couldn't pry any wood loose to build a fire.

Old Mrs. Utsumi managed to milk the cow herself while

her husband was laid up, but her poor old arms was too weak to chop the ice off the woodpile. The only warm thing they had to keep them alive was cow's milk.

So my dad went over and chopped through the ice on their woodpile and built them a big fire in their stove to start with. My mom made them hot food, and my dad took Mr. Utsumi down to River Bend to get a cast on his leg.

Well, since that cold winter went by, Mrs. Utsumi made some embroidery pillowcases for my mom and they always share vegetables from their garden, and plus the iris bulbs Mrs. Utsumi gave my mom.

And if Shazam had said that word right where old Mr. Utsumi could hear her? Oh, Lord.

But then poor Shazam didn't have a father to teach her right from wrong.

And it was because of Japan she didn't have a father.

It would be a terrible thing to lose your very own father forever. But to lose your very own son forever like the Utsumis! Out of all the bad things that could happen, which of those would be the very worst?

The only thing my mom ever said, the whole time, was about Shazam's father himself. And it stunned me. "That child might be better off he's at the bottom of the sea. He can't get himself or nobody else in trouble." I went bug-eyed. She wouldn't say anything more. Hard as I tried, she wouldn't.

Alva, shortstop

Well, I got down on my knees.

Dear God,

Oh what my ma told me, I promised her I wouldn't say a word to anybody, and I'll keep my promise. Like they say, take it to the Lord in prayer.

It is about Shazam's mother. It is too terrible to say.

If it is too terrible to say in front of You, but if You already know about it because You already know everything, then how can both of those things be true? I am always so confused about that. It don't make good sense. But I know I can talk to You about it.

It was after we found out about Shazam's father dying from when she told Hallie, and then Shazam's mother was coming here to visit for Christmas, and my mother just bursted it out to me, she could not hold it in no longer.

Well, You already know. Isn't it awful? Even my ma said, "Poor little thing" about Shazam. Well, I tell You this for sure, I would never in my life say "Poor little thing" about Shazam before. But then I heard this terrible part about her mother.

Her mother. Floy. You know how she was. She did not even finish her high school years because she took to sin. My ma actually said, "She couldn't keep her bloomers on." You know how she got so flirty with that Takashima boy in the berry patch.

Why didn't she stop there God?

Isn't it tragic? How she went down to Portland and she got herself — this is the worst part — when she got herself in the family way by a boy she met? That boy, he had already stole a car once, his name was Buzz? And he tried to brush her off and he went in the Navy, remember that?

And she followed him to his base in San Diego, remember?

Pregnant with child at such a young age!

If You can do anything why didn't You save her from her sin? Isn't that what You are supposed to do?

I'm not blaming You God. I am just asking.

And she named the baby Shirley, after Buzz's mother. Think of that! Imagine if You were a boy and You made a girl have a baby, and then she named the baby after Your very own mother. Wouldn't You marry her then? Just for naming the baby? Well, this Buzz the car stealer would not.

Well, then when her mother sent her some money to go all the way to Honolulu, Buzz said they would get married if she went there.

So she went there, I guess they got married. Child and all.

And then Japan bombed Pearl Harbor and he was on his ship, the *Arizona,* and kerplooey, the ship sunk to smithereens. No more Buzz.

Poor Shazam. Her mother a sinner and her crook father dead. No wonder she gets so tangled in her face.

Wouldn't that make anybody a problem child God?

My ma would not of told me if she didn't have a sad place in her heart for that poor orphan girl of sin. My ma she kept the secret from the day Shazam showed up here till now. It just come tumbling out of her when she found out Floy came here for Christmas to be with her daughter and her mother out there by the gravel pit in their little puny house with no indoor plumbing. My ma she shook her head with pity.

How will I keep this bad secret and not tell no one?

In a way, everybody should know about it, so they could all be understanding to Shazam. In another way, nobody should know because of her shame. If nobody knows, nobody can call her bad names for her parents not being married when she was had by her mother.

I don't think Shazam knows all that bad part. About how Floy couldn't keep her bloomers on. Your own mother would never tattle such a thing on herself, would she? How could Shazam stay alive if she knew?

But still, she is a odd one for sure. But if I keep remembering that secret gossip I will be nice to her from pity in my heart.

I wonder if Coach Rayfield knows about Floy. He keeps saying Shazam has not had opportunities like us. And he says she has the determination of a good sports athlete, and he says also we need to be thankful for 2 things: 1, she come here to play us a great game next May, and 2, she come here to teach us niceness to a person so different.

Now that is the end of my talking about Shazam and her tragedy.

Next. Thank You for making me ever getting better at pivoting to be the best shortstop I can be. I even work on it sometimes when we go in the big indoor room for our little weensie practices.

I know You didn't make the 3rd-grade teacher break her leg slipping in the dead raccoon guts on her back porch and get a cast put on so she hobbles with a crutch. But I know You made her ask me would I do chores for her such as getting her book sack and taking it in the school from her car parked at the maple tree swing. And her violin case on Thursdays for music day. And You made her tell me I should always be ready to help her exactly when the bell rings for both recesses and after school and also be there at 7:43 A.M. at her car to help her with her things. I know You told her I would be worth 30¢ every school day just to help her. I know You wanted me to get a good glove so I can be a good shortstop.

I will be able to get my glove with my money I earn from Miss James. I have helped her every school day, I even went over there on a Christmas vacation day to clean her floor for her. She was playing on her violin sitting down. Lucky I didn't get the chicken pox, I had them last year.

Thank You God.

Next. Thank You for making me do good in playing Mary in the Christmas play. I was honored to be chose and I rode the donkey quite good and did not slide off. And the donkey did not poop even one time in the church, it has been Mary's donkey so many Christmases. Thank You for that. When we had the manger scene I stayed very still with the baby Jesus. I did not notice Shazam just plain walked out of the play till later when the others told me she did so. How come she did that God? How could a shepherd just walk right off the hillside when Jesus was born in a manger?

But it was a very good Christmas play anyway.

Thank You for listening to my prayers all the time God. I appreciate it.

Next. There is my ma and dad, I told You about before. Could You please help my dad get that tractor job he needs? And my ma's missing tooth over on the side where she laughs, could You help my dad get that job so she can go to the dentist? It is so embarrassing, other mothers do not have a missing tooth. During good weather when my dad is logging we get along fine, but in the winter the woods is all snowed in up there. So he needs that job.

I know my ma had Your guidance and everlasting help to sew that pretty pink comforter for my Christmas present, doing it when I was gone or asleep so I never did know she was making me it. I am grateful for it.

"Leaning on the everlasting arms," it is such a good

church song, and I know exactly how it means in my heart. Thank You God.

Would You maybe help Shazam not be so strange? I am just asking.

Thy will be done, Amen.

But just think. Her dad would not be in heaven, would he? For stealing a car and doing pregnancy to her mother Floy? But he would be in heaven for dying for his country. So what would be fair and where is her dad's soul?

Your friend,
Alva

Shazam, center field

I left that Christmas play in the church I couldnt breathe in there.

Kate and Little Peggy

Kate, second base

I was never so excited in my entire whole life before, it was a real refrigerator. Right in our kitchen.

It plugs into the new electric we got. That Christmas was the first time we ever had automatic light with switches on the wall. No more kerosene lamps. I could turn on my light beside my bed in the middle of the night if I woke up. It is called rural electrification.

It was the most excitement of my life, even more than every time my mother had another little brother.

The refrigerator makes cubes of ice in the top. You pour water into the metal tray and there's a part with squares, well, cubes, really, cube shapes. It's a rack thing. You put it in the tray. You put the tray full of water in the freezer box in the top of the refrigerator and you take it out the next morning and the water is completely frozen, and you pull up a lever on the tray and lift out ice in cubes.

We gave our old icebox to the church.

My folks were so proud we got this new refrigerator, my mom kept cooking things and putting them in the fridge, we call it. Macaroni and cheese. Salmon loaf. And the tomato aspic does not go bad.

No more blocks of ice for us, I hated when we had to bring it up from River Bend or even just down to the crick in winter. The ice dripped all over and I always had to be the one to mop the puddles off the floor.

I wondered why my dad was so different about getting the ice from the crick on Christmas Eve day before we had to go up to the church. He was saying, "I just love hauling this ice up from the crick, I just love hauling it. Don't you just love hauling it?" He said to two of my brothers which were holding the sheets of ice on the sled going up the hill.

"No no no no no," my brothers complained the whole trip up the hill. "How come we have to do it on Christmas Eve?" went my one brother, and my other brother said swear words, I heard him through the trees.

And then on Christmas morning we were having our presents and I wondered how come our presents were so small ones, like only socks and no pretty sweater like I wanted. I was almost getting how my mom calls pouty, and my dad said, "Let's see if Santa left anything on the back porch," on account of my littlest brother still believes in Santa. He made us go out there in our slippers and pajamas and sure enough. The huge enormous box with a red ribbon bow on top.

And inside it our fridge. Our very own.

It seemed to be a miracle.

We made fudge on the day after Christmas and we didn't even have to let it harden up on the porch. The next day we made Kool-Aid ice cubes.

It was the most amazing thing, we never had anything like it.

It made me more like the others. Susannah has a fridge because her dad is a doctor and her mother is a nurse and they have to keep medicines in it. And they are a little bit rich, besides, they have somebody completely outside their family to come and clean their house. And Shadean has a fridge because her dad has two orchards. And Ellen has one on account of the G.I. Bill from the government. And Little Peggy too and Daisy and Tootie. Even Lorelei's poor family has one.

So there was only Aki, their poor house looked so decrepitated on the outside. After they were gone for so long and the McHenrys rented it out, Aki's family didn't have hardly anything, I doubted they had a fridge. I would never ask her, it was too embarrassing. And back then we never went over to Aki's house, she never invited us.

And Vernell does not have one, they are so poor down there in the swale with their scrawny goats.

Our new refrigerator. I loved saying it. Refrigerator.

My mom was the most thrilled of anybody. I have always gotten real tired of my mom and dad making sure we count our blessings every day on account of how poor they were when they were kids. My mom always reminds me which I do not need reminding of her not even having one dress when she was little. And only shoes that got too small for her brothers. And she did not get to finish her eighth grade of school. Whenever I complain about anything — about honestly anything — my mom says, "Quit your bellyaching and count your dresses."

Even when she went with the Ladies Aid to help pack up the 11 boxes of Christmas food for the poor, she said how they weren't as poor like she was when she was little. She is so proud of Dad he is a logger and there is many advantages on account of many house builders needing wood all the time.

Well, that Christmas, with our new electrical lights and specially our refrigerator I was sure I would count my blessings forever. My mom made the prettiest orange layered fruit cocktail Jell-O salad I ever saw to take to the church potluck and pageant. It was the favorite salad of anybody's. I ate a ton of food so I was almost too full to be a good angel in the pageant.

Christmas was good in many ways. When the pond behind McHenrys' froze and they rigged up a light on the back of the store for night skating, we all went there and I saw Mr.

and Mrs. Porter holding hands on the ice, it was so romantic. They met each other in the war, I would love to meet a soldier and have him love me. They are good skaters together, like a movie. Mrs. Porter skated over to Daisy and me and said, "Are you girls at least *think*ing about hitting, catching, and throwing?" Me and Daisy got embarrassed. Then she said, "Well, are you at least *think*ing about arithmetic?" I confess I didn't think very much about playing ball or doing school. The whole ball field was 2 foot deep under snow.

And when school started again after New Year's, there was Tuesdays when I didn't get to do the indoor drills on account of it being my milking day.

The point is: I thought that refrigerator was the most important thing of the year I was 11. It was not the most important thing. The most important thing was still invisible but it was right close by and I didn't even suspect.

Little Peggy, right field

Beginning in sixth grade I had a best friend; I had not exactly had one before. Aki came here, and we turned into best friends, it just happened. It might have been partly because we're both short and we got to be fire drill partners, partly because Mrs. Porter arranged our seats together, and partly because it was OK with me that she was so quiet about things. We felt like best friends, being together. We fitted.

The only really odd thing about her was that she wouldn't eat potatoes. Even the cook at school would always let her know the day before she was making potato soup, so Aki would bring her lunch.

Aki has eyes shaped like petals of a daisy.

In the class picture we two are standing right behind Jerry McHenry and Piper, who are kneeling on their knees with their hair uncombed. Aki had slept over with me the night before, and we were wearing each other's blouses.

We always slept over at my house, never at Aki's. She never invited me. Her house couldn't get fixed up all at once, with harvest and everything. We never talked about it, it was just the way it was.

Aki was kind of a mystery in that way. In the things she didn't say. We all told about our childhoods, things like that. She hardly ever told anything.

And she wouldn't say a word about the bad things that happened to her and her family all those years. Not even to me. In fact, when somebody wrote the nasty words about Japanese people on McHenrys' Store window with soap in the night, and Mr. McHenry himself was out there washing them off in the morning when our school bus went past, Aki acted like she didn't see the writing. How could she not see it? It was huge.

Some of the boys on the bus said, "Look over there at McHenrys' window." Aki could not have not seen it.

But she turned her head completely away and put her books in her arms, ready to get off the bus across the road at the school.

If my parents didn't tell me all what terrible things happened to Aki and her whole family, I wouldn't even know about how they got sent away from their home and everything.

We were going to be shepherds together in the Christmas play. But when I had to miss it because of having chicken pox, Aki was able to keep my sheep calm during the whole manger scene, everybody said so. She had some special whispers she whispered to it and it just stood there being respectful to Jesus, that's how well she was able to gentle it.

I had to miss the whole church potluck and pageant and everything. But both Vernell and Aki volunteered to save my Christmas bag, so I got it eventually. Every bag is always the same: McHenrys' Store gives the candy cane and the orange; the filberts and walnuts come from the trees behind the church; and our school principal's husband makes his Christmas fudge and wraps a piece for everybody's bag. The Christmas bags are only for kids under twelve, so we will never get them again.

And then there was what happened with the Valentine cookies.

It was Shadean's idea to bake Valentine cookies for our whole grade and also for the old men gathered around the woodstove at McHenrys' Store.

Not only does Shadean's dad have a new tractor, her

mother has a new electric stove. So naturally we did the baking at her house.

We baked all day Sunday afternoon after church, because Valentine's Day happened on a Monday this year. Daisy came over after her Catholic church down at River Bend, and Lorelei's father brought Vernell from down at her house in the swale, so everybody was there.

It was that Sunday afternoon when Kate and Vernell were playing band director with their knives dipped in frosting and the red frosting splashed on Aki's skirt that they realized they had gone too far. Shadean tried washing it off with Ivory Flakes, but it just smeared worse.

Aki couldn't just have a new skirt any time her old one got messed up. And when we saw what that reckless playing had done to Aki's skirt, we were all ashamed that we let it happen. Aki's skirt was white and gray stripes like you'd see in a man's suit for church. I think her mother or grandmother made it, but Aki did not say so. Shadean's mother told Aki to take off the skirt and she'd soap it up, and we all went to Shadean's room to find another skirt for Aki to wear.

Shadean pulled open her closet door; it sounded whishy over the new carpet she has in her room. The carpet is blue and it looks so good with her ruffle curtains that she and her mother sewed on their new Singer machine. Shadean lives in a house of luxury.

We looked in her closet and Aki said, "Oh, you have so much clothes," in that soft, exact voice of hers. Shadean has

8 skirts that fit her, we counted. We found one for Aki that was not too much too big. It is a brown one.

"You can have that skirt if you want it," Shadean said. "I don't care."

"Oh, no, I'll bring it back," Aki said, and she put it on.

Aki always said no to things; it was her way. No, I'm not such a good ball player (she was too), No, I don't always get a hundred on my spelling tests (she did too), No, I don't draw birds best in our grade (she did too). Now it was no to having Shadean's skirt. Everybody knew Shadean had too many skirts and Aki didn't have enough.

We got all the Valentines decorated with faces and hearts and some birds and flowers, and our final count was 68 cookies.

We all moaned with our stomachs too full of the frosting.

The next day when Mrs. Porter let us go across the road and take Valentine's cookies to the old men at the woodstove in McHenrys' Store, those old men were so thankful, two of them said they would take us home and have us cook for them. Mr. McHenry himself walked us back across the road to school because the snowplow had heaped the piles so high he was worried we couldn't see if a car might be coming.

And then Susannah's mother had the greatest idea, which Susannah told when Aki was home with chicken pox. Aki still had no first baseman's glove of her own and the only one for a lefty in the sports cupboard was old and raggedy. Susannah's mother suggested why don't we all chip in and get Aki a nifty glove for her birthday? As a surprise. Everybody in the class. This would include Jerry McHenry, Darrell and Donald, Piper, Herby, and everybody.

It was a unanimous vote. I guess Aki was the only girl in the class that every single boy would vote for. She never did anything to make any of them mad. In fact, she never did anything to make anybody mad.

They elected me treasurer of the collection for Aki's glove. Shadean and Mrs. Porter chose the perfect one, a Spalding Trapper.

Everybody was supposed to bring in 50¢ for the glove. There were some who wouldn't remember, like Donald or Vernell, and Mrs. Porter put in whatever money was missing. It had to be a secret till Aki's birthday in April.

The terrible thing is that I didn't read the invisible signs. I should have. The skirt, the writing on McHenrys' window. Even Aki's niceness all the time. Even that. The way she never made a fuss about anything. If anybody could have read the signs, it should have been me.

Instead, I would wake in the middle of the night sometimes, worrying that I wouldn't play well enough in our Bat 6. I would lie in bed and concentrate on being able to throw over to first or second. Or I'd worry that somebody might spill the beans about Aki's mitt before her birthday. I would lie there and listen to fir-tree branches unloading their heavy snow. It sounded like a comforter falling off a bed.

Lola and Lila, Shazam, and Wink

Lola and Lila, managers and general subs

It was so much fun at Wink's birthday party on January 1st, New Year's Day. We all had pretty dresses and there was such good games. Her mom makes excellent birthday parties, and the cake is always the BEST. Wink shoveled the path from the driveway to their porch by herself, all the 8 inches of new snow from the night before. It was that big heavy wet snow that breaks fruit tree branches. Manny and Alva rode with us due to both of their cars were stuck in the snow that day.

Wink invited Shazam because she would feel bad leaving her out. Shazam's mother came to visit her for Christmas from over in Idaho where she got a job. Darlene's parents went to pick her up at the Greyhound. She brought Shazam a fancy green satin dress for Christmas, and that was a goofy gift because Shazam didn't even have good boots to wear in the snow till the Gospel Church ladies bought her a pair. A fancy green shiny dress with puffed sleeves was ridiculous.

Shazam came to Wink's party wearing that bright fancy dress and we all just stood there not knowing what to say and Wink's mother said, "Oh, Shirley, your dress is real pretty, you look real pretty, doesn't she?" And of course we were birthday party visitors so we had to make pretend, and we all said Yes your dress is real pretty. It was a pretty dress, but for in a movie, not for in real life.

Everybody was over the chicken pox for Wink's party. We did not get the chicken pox till January 4 (Lola) and then January 11 (Lila).

Shazam didn't get chicken pox. She promised she never had them in her life. Her grandmother told the principal she didn't know if Shazam ever had the pox or not. *"Not know?"* we said. "How could you *not know* if somebody ever had them?"

Our mom said, "*Some*body should know. That girl's mother should know."

But when Shazam's mother came to visit her own daughter for Christmas, she didn't even remember. That's what Shazam said, "My mom don't remember if I had them."

Wink was so in love with Hank Greenberg, her baseball hero of the Detroit Tigers, she made a pin the bat on the ball game instead of pin the tail on the donkey. It was going too far, but we went along with it.

Shazam tilted her head way back so she could see under

the blindfold. And Wink's mother said at the very start of the game, "Now, we don't want no peekers," she said it to everybody. But Shazam peeked and she got the prize, a snow globe, a shaker-thing with water inside a glass ball and Santa Claus and a house, and you shake it and the snow falls down.

Wink's mother pretended Shazam didn't tilt her head way back and peek out from under the bandanna. She gave her the prize anyway. We had good manners not to say anything. I was going to (Lola), but I poked her not to (Lila). Three other people saw it and nobody said a word. We were being very good sports about Shazam coming in and taking over the place on the team that would have gone to me (Lola). Every time we turned around we had to be good sports on account of Shazam.

Shazam looked at the prize wondering what it was. Then Wink went over to her and she said very mannerly down to her from her tall height, "Give it a shake." And Shazam shakes it and the snow swirled around and her face went surprised. She never saw one of those usual objects before in her life.

Wink and her mother both, they made her birthday cake together, it was chocolate inside and it had pure white boiled icing standing up in Mt. Hood peaks all over it, and the 12 candle holders were all different colors like flowers. And Wink blew out every one of the candles on one breath.

At the end of the party she showed us the birthday present her mom made for her. It was a professional jersey for our Bat game and it had a great big number 5 on the back, just like Hank Greenberg on the Detroit Tigers, which is Wink's birthday twin and her loverboy hero.

The Barlow General Store kept their Christmas tree up till 4 days after Wink's party. The needles fell all over the canned goods and Brita Marie had to do cleanup. Her dad paid her.

The old men that sit at the woodstove in the store with the lame dog said this wasn't the worst winter they remembered, it was way worse some other years. One of them that was in France in the war said us children never saw such a winter like they had over there.

Men always talk about the wars, ladies always say let's forget the fighting.

We had 2 days of bare roads and Coach Rayfield had us go running before it snowed again. We had to run on the road that goes in front of the school, on up to where the fenced alfalfa field starts, and we had to round the corner fast, making sure we put our foot on the orange paint splotch on the road. We had to go all the way around behind the gray barn where the back road comes in, then way down to the Flying Horse gas station and back to the school. Where the gravel was slidy you could fall, lots of us had fallen, Audrey fell and her knee was so bloody she got it all over Darlene and Ila Mae who was helping her walk back down the road. Other times Coach made us run all the way past the goat woman's house clear to the creek and back.

Coach Rayfield meets us on the home stretch and runs the last part with us. He yells at us, "You got to have endurance. That distance between bases gets real, real long when you got a fast outfielder. You're gonna feel real, real bad when that ball beats you to the base. You tired, Shazam?"

"Yeah," she says, puffing.

"You gonna keep on running, Shazam?"

"Yeah," she says, puffing.

He wanted everybody to have endurance like Shazam. And us 2 were extras besides.

Us 2 went through the whole long winter without fighting even once about who had to crack through the ice in the dog's dish in the mornings or about doing the ironing. Not once. For a reward we got new powder-blue angora sweaters for a Valentine gift, and there was lots of time left to wear them before the weather turned warm.

Shazam, center field

You never know one of them might sneak up behind your back like they done my dad I saw them. You always got to keep your eye out.

Wink, first base

Here is what I thought:

1. We had a good group of 6th-grade girls and some OK boys too, we were lucky to be growing up in a nice place.

2. It was fun being a wise man in the Christmas pageant, carrying the box of frankincense to the manger. Despite of what they say, it is all right for a girl to be a wise man, I am tall enough to be a good one. Ila Mae's middle brother and Billy Shimatsu's big brother and me did very good in bringing our presents, we all walked together and we none of us tripped over anything.

3. I had a almost perfect party, on my birthday I share with my twin, the first baseman Hank Greenberg on the Detroit Tigers.

4. I was so lucky to be the owner of Beautiful Hair's sister's super glove from when she was Most Valuable Player in 1945, she got it from their aunt that had it before the war. It is a antique glove and it was broke in so good and it is a historical object. I was so glad I did her chores for her all those weeks, even feeding their chickens and weeding the lettuce and radishes and peas over at their house. I earned that glove and I believed it would bring me good luck. I offered her money for her good-luck socks she wore when she played her Bat 6, but she would not sell them to me.

5. I had been practicing sliding into base more than anybody else, I was the only one good at it. Ila Mae and some others only half-tried, they didn't get down like me. Coach Rayfield agreed I could wear slacks on May 28. In the snowy

weather I actually had daydreams of sliding into base and winning our game.

6. But we might not win. I knew we would have disappointments in our lifes. I learned about disappointments from my birthday twin Hank Greenberg, the great first baseman on the Detroit Tigers of the American League.

Here was his disappointment. He was driving in his car listening to the car radio and he heard he was not a Detroit Tiger anymore, he had been sent to play for the Pittsburgh team which are the Pirates, in a total different league, the National League.

I thought about that disappointment of his life. And I promised I would be able to go through disappointments in my life, learning from Hank.

In the 1945 World Series he hit a grand slam home run in the 9th inning and he won the Series for Detroit. He was the Most Valuable Player 2 times, in 1935 and in 1940.

I was thinking how Hank is Jewish by his race and he is as good as any Gentile like me which is a Christian. It is inside what counts, if you try to be good like Jesus and if you have heaven in your heart.

Hank Greenberg is also very tall for his age like me. He is 6 feet and 3½ inches in heighth and I am 5 feet and 10 inches. He went to fight for his country in the war. He went to China in a B-29. And lucky for me he came back alive. Hank batted in 138 runs in the year 1937. He hit 2 home runs in the same game 11 times in the year of 1938.

But even so he did not win all the time. Life is not all winning.

And that made me think of the next thing.

7. Shazam was a very queer girl it is true. She had a sadder life than us. There was such a bad scandal about her mother I wouldn't even say the words. And Shazam got real strange from having such terribleness. Therefore it was my philosophy on life that she might of been put here to test our goodness. God might be wondering if we could be good Christians even with Shazam in our midst like. She even put down her shepherd's crook and walked right out of the Christmas pageant, it was crazy for a shepherd to just up and leave the hillside. We were lucky Ila Mae moved right in to fill up the empty space. It did not ruin the pageant.

And every time I looked at Lola I saw how she had to give up her hope of being a starting player for Barlow for 1949 and she would remember it for the rest of her life. And all because of Shazam coming here.

8. I voted everything would turn out OK and we had to be nice to Shazam. Like Coach said, Shazam was one of us now, and odd like she was she still deserved to be treated by the Golden Rule like everybody else.

And besides, Shazam did not look so surprised all the time when you talked to her anymore, like before when she first came here she looked like you had caught her off her guard whenever you asked her something. By the time I was thinking this list of thoughts she was more used to us.

9. And also, there is Jackie Robinson on the Brooklyn Dodgers, he is even a *Negro.* He was Rookie of the Year for 1947 and he stole more bases than anybody. In a way, that was even stranger than Shazam.

10. Spring was coming, there was only about a foot of snow left on our ball field. Darlene's dad that drove the snowplow part-time did not even go out to work for five days after my birthday.

11. Who was going to win that game?

Susannah and Aki

Susannah, left field

I mainly have some things to tell about Aki because I was there and nobody else was. I was the first one that found out what mean things were still happening, even long after the war was over and everything was supposed to be normal.

Aki never told these important things about herself, so somebody else has to. Including the reason why she didn't get back to her home till time for 6th grade, when she belonged here from the very beginning.

It is because my dad is the doctor that I found out. Otherwise they might have kept it a complete secret.

Aki's father and Jerry McHenry's father were boys in school together. In McHenrys' Store on the wall of the office in the back is a photograph of them in old-fashioned clothes standing beside a little short dogwood tree that is now so huge and enormous it has to be pruned so children can get in the door of the school. Aki's mother was a schoolgirl here too. And she was Most Valuable Player in the Bat of 1930.

Aki's father took over his father's orchard when he got grown up, and Aki was a baby here just the same as the rest of us. But her whole family got sent away to a camp for the whole time the war was on. Only us children didn't even know about the camps, I think our parents tried to keep a lot of the bad things of the war away from us. We only found out later.

We were going into third grade when the war got over in 1945. We were too young to catch onto it very much, but when it got over there was a whole crowd of people cheering all over the road in front of McHenrys' Store and my mom and me were there, Kate and her mom were there too, I remember her red braids bouncing when we jumped up and down, the big tall crowd of people were celebrating.

So the Japanese got out of the camps they had been sent to, and they could start their free lives again. Some of the families came back here and others did not. And I know why.

One night in the middle of the night my dad had to go to the Shimatsus' house down in Barlow, a brick had gotten thrown through their window and hit their baby in his crib. Some white person threw a brick at a baby.

And the war had already gotten over.

And the reason why. The reason why is that they just didn't like the Japanese at all.

My parents didn't want to tell me, they thought I was too

young to understand. But they couldn't not tell me when I already knew about the middle of the night and the brick and the baby. *Then* my dad explained that many people did not like the Japanese for many years, even long before the war. For one thing, the Japanese were such hard workers. The whole family would work many more hours each day, that is their custom. By working so hard, they can make bad soil have good crops, and white farmers got mad at them for it, they didn't like the competition.

There were often signs and writing in soap on windows saying Japanese not wanted here, things like that.

That little baby had to have stitches in the side of his face. Doesn't it make your skin crawl?

My father had to make the stitches.

Well, Lorelei's father wrote an angry letter to the newspaper down in River Bend about that. He always writes angry letters to the newspaper. It is probably very hard for Lorelei with her father being like that.

So, Aki's parents knew there were some people with bad feelings about Japanese people around here. The newspaper down in River Bend announced Japanese people might have bad things done to them if they came back. And it came true, that bad thing happened to the Shimatsus' baby with that brick. The Mikamis wanted to keep Aki and her brother Shig away from such nasty things. So when they got out of the camp and could go free, they tried to live other places. But they got homesick for their orchard.

So they came back. Aki's dad and mom, and Aki's old grandmother, who doesn't hardly speak any English, and Aki and her brother Shig, which is in high school at the Consolidated.

And Aki turned up by surprise, and so did her softball-champion mother. Aki's mother told my mother confidentially: They wanted Aki to get to play the Bat in her only year to do it in her life, that is one reason they came back.

There. I finally got to tell that part.

We were all so sure it was such a good thing for our team Aki came back. I was such a shaky player, I even felt jittery trying on my Mountaineer cap. My friend Darlene played on the Barlow Pioneers team, her mom cleans for my mom, I knew it would feel odd playing against her. But me and Darlene had seen it coming. Everybody knew that in 6th grade you play against each other to learn good sportsmanship and get ready to be 7th graders together at the Consolidated.

I don't feel better after telling it, even though I was waiting all this long time for my turn.

Aki, first base

I didn't want to take a turn at all. I thought it would be better if I let the other girls tell it. Then Peggy especially told me it wouldn't only be not fair, it wouldn't even be true if I didn't do my part. Maybe she's right.

So I'll go next.

It was the cherry tree swing, mainly. My father constructed a swing when I was very small, and he hung it in the cherry tree closest to our house, and I swung on it all the time when we lived here in Bear Creek Ridge. Even though much of those old days was fuzzy in my memory for a long time, it's clear now. I clearly remember my brother Shig pushing me in the swing when my feet couldn't even come close to touching the ground.

My father made it to swing very straight; it doesn't swerve off to the side like many I've swung on.

I would sit in my little childhood swing and put my elbows around the ropes and lean back and look up into the cherry tree. When I sat very still the jays flew screeching from branch to branch to branch, fluttering up the robins from their perches and making a big fuss. Sometimes a leaf dropped, making no sound. In blossom time petals fell on the ground around me. Sometimes they fell on me. In a way, I guess I was never so happy.

I have tried to set things in order lately. They were so jumbled, I couldn't tell which things came first. But now I think the swing was first.

And then next, my grandmother, who has always spoken Japanese, almost no English, kept walking back and forth in the house, back and forth across the linoleum, and I walked with her. I thought it was a game.

She kept saying, *Shikata ga nai, shikata ga nai.* And I said it back to her, and she picked me up and held me close to her and walked back and forth in the house carrying me and we were singing together:

Shikata ga nai, shikata ga nai.

This saying generally means don't make a fuss, there is nothing to be done, you can't help what is happening.

I thought it was a song, but my grandmother was explaining to me that we had to go away.

As first I didn't understand anything about why we were going away. Even later there were so many things I didn't understand.

We left Bear Creek Ridge on May 13, 1942. Maybe it was the next day after my grandmother and I walked back and forth, or maybe it was two or three days after. Naturally, I didn't know this date till later, because I was too young to understand a calendar.

We rode on a train. The window shades in the train had to be closed, it was a rule of some kind. No one was supposed to look out the window, and I guess no one was supposed to see in. Someone tied a number tag to the buttonhole of my coat and I went to sleep and woke up in a completely different place, not my home.

And every face I saw there was Japanese but the soldiers were not. The soldiers were keeping us safe, I was told.

I wanted to swing in the swing my father had made, but we had gone away, and the grownups were so busy trying to do arrangements for us to eat and sleep, nobody listened to me about the swing.

It's silly now to think of, but I honestly didn't know where the swing had gone. For years I remembered the small details of the ropes going up high and the wooden seat under my legs.

This childish swing in the cherry tree was a mystery to me for so long.

We stayed in one crowded place for some time, I don't know how long, and then we moved again and stayed for more than three years in a camp in the desert.

I thought we had gone away from America. Actually, we were still in America, but I didn't know that. I was so little I didn't ask that question. So of course no one answered it.

I didn't really think it through all the way, but the tag someone had tied to a buttonhole on my coat must have seemed like a ticket to go to another country.

I clearly remember my mom holding me warm in bed with some coats piled heavy on top of us when we were in camp. The stove in the barracks smelled bad and the wind blew icy cold in winter. My mom brushed the sand out of my hair, and she shampooed it, but sand always got in again, it was always in the wind. There is no wind like it here.

We had one room for our family, but we didn't eat our meals there. We ate in the mess hall, and the waiting lines were long. We passed the time playing jacks or hopscotch, and some older children taught me to play cat's cradle with string. There were many children to play with all the time. It was so noisy in the mess hall, my grandmother would just hold her head in her hands and close her eyes. She would often say in Japanese, "Oh, potatoes. Oh, potatoes. Who grows these many tasteless potatoes? Oh, potatoes." I agreed with her after a long while.

Even though my father made a rock garden in front of the barracks, it was never a home, although all those years I thought it was our home. I got very mixed up about what home is.

We had reading lessons in my cousins' barracks with "See Dick and Jane run." After we learned to read we had "See Ko run" and "See Min run" and "See Aki run" games outside, between the barracks.

It feels as if we played ball every day, but maybe that is just a trick of my memory. By the time I was eight years old I had played every position on our team, and had subbed on other teams when I was needed. One time I slid into second base and got a bad abrasion on my left leg. It was oozy and I had to sit and watch my cousins and everybody else play till my leg healed. The weather was hot and dusty, and my mom washed the dirt out of my abrasion even though I would rather have the dirt stay in there because the washing hurt.

The big kids coached us, and the grownups, too. Now that I am older, I realize the grownups coached us so they wouldn't be idle in camp. There was nothing much for them to do. They could work in the bakery or at other jobs. But those jobs were both tiring and boring. So we had many coaches.

The guard in the watchtower, who stood there all day

long to make sure no one escaped, said my team was his favorite. He said we were the pluckiest. He could look down on the camp and see many teams play. My brother Shig and his friends called him Fatty behind his back. I don't know why he liked us the most. We were just little kids.

All of us had to learn to write the things we did in our games. When I was six years old I learned to spell "shortstop," "batting average," "inning," and other game words. Our older cousins were our teachers and those were their favorite words to make us learn.

Later I learned that first graders don't have to spell those words. Many first graders can only spell their names.

I learned to read and do arithmetic up to long division. Our teachers had us say the Pledge of Allegiance every day. And we had handwriting practice and drawing lessons and we also had a children's chorus. And then eventually we left the camp because the war was over. I suddenly had to say good-bye to those many friends I had made. I don't know where they all went, Ko, Min, and the many other children I had played with.

I thought we were going back to America. We went to two places in California and stayed there a long time. I went to fourth and fifth grade there. My cousins and I voted not to eat potatoes ever again.

While we were in California someone wrote bad words about us on my uncle's car with paint. It washed almost all off but I can still see those words in my mind.

And it was in California that we kids started trying not to be Japanese. I don't remember exactly where we got that idea. One day my girl cousins and I put makeup on our eyes to make them round, and if you stood far enough away we didn't look Japanese at all. We took turns going halfway down the block and looking. Then my cousin Kazuko tried to change her name to Sally. And we started to have a bake sale to earn money to buy hair bleach. My aunts put an end to that.

The worst part was my aunts and my mom crying when they found out.

My mother got so upset. She whispered with anger at me: "What if your grandmother saw you do these things? You would break her heart!"

I hadn't thought about that. I have seen my grandmother sit with her shoulders hunched over, not saying anything for long, long periods of time. At camp and at the places where we went later. She was so unhappy. She is old and it is hard for her to change places of living so many times. But I hadn't thought about her heart breaking because we kids wanted to fit in better in California.

And still I kept missing the swing, not knowing where it had gone because of my confusion of memory. Every time I asked when we would go back to the United States, my parents said we are already in the United States, and they kept pointing out flags.

I still didn't get it.

I meant when would we go back to the place where the swing was. But my parents didn't know which swing I wanted to go back to, because there had been swings in the different places where we lived. My dad helped make swings in camp for the children, and then there were swings in Sacramento where we lived with our cousins.

I meant the cherry tree swing in Bear Creek Ridge, but I didn't know how to say all three words of the name of the place I meant. Eventually I stopped asking, because it sounded so childish. My parents didn't even mention Bear Creek Ridge because they were thinking we would never come back here at all.

The McHenrys had sent my parents news from the newspaper saying there were signs that said "No Japs or Dogs" in windows of some stores down at River Bend. And the newspaper from River Bend itself said we should not come back. It was not on every page of the newspaper, just on some pages. When the McHenrys sent us this information they said we were wanted in Bear Creek Ridge but there were some people who were still keeping their old feelings from the war. The McHenrys said, "We just want you to know it will be hard on you when you come back, you should know the truth of how things are here." And they wrote in the letters how our orchard was doing, and it wasn't doing very well, due to the McHenrys' not being able to take careful care of the trees along with their own orchards too, as well as the store.

My parents took a long time to decide.

I even dreamed about the cherry-blossom petals floating down onto my lap. But we had been so many places, the place in the dream seemed to be nowhere that existed in real life. With all the different places added up, it was six years that I wanted to come back to that swing in the United States.

And when we came back to our own house last summer, it was hard to remember our home. Everything was overgrown with weeds, and our house was a very bad mess because the McHenrys had rented it to some people who were not careful. And the roof of the garage was caved in. The orchard had not been pruned or thinned or sprayed regularly, and the coddling moths had done much damage. My father and mother were so sad and angry, it was terrible to watch their disappointed faces.

The McHenrys brought us seven boxes of groceries and other things from their store to welcome us back and my mother did not want to accept them but it was in neighborly goodwill. And she was glad there were baking powder and butter and sugar and three new mixing bowls to replace the ones that the renters threw against the kitchen wall in their drinking fights. In one box there were even new saddle shoes, exactly my size.

And from the church there were towels and a tablecloth, plus jars of canned fruits and vegetables from everyone who joined in.

And there was the swing, exactly where I remembered it,

hanging from the cherry tree, and green moss had grown on the wooden seat and the ropes were green with moss too. I went very carefully to the swing and I sat very still in it. I'd grown so much that the swing was way too close to the ground for me. Then I pushed off with my feet and pumped myself high up in the tree where the ripening cherries were hanging in clusters. I was never so glad to be anywhere in my life.

The cherry tree had grown much taller. Looking up into it, I felt I was a different person but yet the same person who had swung in it long before.

Our house was so wrecked it was almost not able to be lived in. My father and my brother set up blankets over the clothesline for a tent, and we all slept outdoors on those first few nights. The Hirokos sent a crate of strawberries home with me on my first afternoon of picking, along with a quart of cream from their cow. My mother rinsed the berries and put them in bowls and poured the cream over them. Our whole family sat on the ground in front of our house and ate berries and cream, and they were so delicious, we were quiet for some length of time, just eating.

My grandmother held her bowl of fresh strawberries in her hands and said, "We are back in the United States."

That was when I met Tootie, in Hirokos' berry patch, and she said I had to be first baseman in Bat 6, and she embarrassed me with talking about how I could help our team win, and about my mother being MVP when she was a girl. I was so happy to have a friend just jump out of the berry rows, and it turned out we used to know each other before we were old enough to walk. And then we started school, and Peggy invited me over to her house and we became good friends.

When we were making cookies at Shadean's house, my eyes were caught by her stuffed panda in her bedroom. It suddenly came back to me: I seemed to remember having a stuffed panda, too. In the years that had gone by I had lost all thoughts of this bear. When I went home that afternoon, wearing Shadean's skirt, I asked my mother if I had really had a stuffed panda, or if I just thought I had.

She remembered that I did. It was probably lost in the confusion of going away, she said. So many things were lost at that time, she said. "And besides," she remembered, "you had taken it to the swing with you so often, it was so dirty from falling on the ground."

And suddenly it came back to me. Not only the swing. The swing and the bear. The swing and the bear and the cherry tree. All three of those things.

"And it wasn't really your favorite toy," my mom said. "It was just a bear. And dirty."

She didn't know. Nobody knew. It was my very own bear.

Nobody suggested to me about forgetting Japanese words. It was my own idea. I would lie in my bed and try to forget them. I would imagine putting them into a bag and tossing them away into the garbage.

And yet my grandmother would always ask me how my day at school had been and had I learned important things. And I couldn't answer her in English if she was to understand me. So I kept changing my plan. I decided to forget all Japanese except the words I would use with my grandmother. But that wasn't practical either, because she often would not use a word for weeks and then she would speak it. I couldn't keep track of what I was supposed to be forgetting.

And it was actually quite hard to forget words. I didn't realize how hard it would be. Lying in my bed at night, I would say the English names for the things in my room, over and over again. I tried to push the Japanese names out of the edges of my mind, and still they kept coming back.

In April, a gigantic surprise came at my birthday. Peggy and her mother made me a birthday cake, chocolate with white coconut icing and twelve candles and my name in rainbow-colored frosting. I couldn't figure out why Peggy wasn't coming outside for afternoon recess. Her mother was bringing the cake to school right then, I saw her carrying a box but didn't think it had anything like a birthday cake in it. When we came back inside from recess, Mrs. Porter and Peggy and Vernell had everything arranged for a party.

They had put up streamers in green-and-white Mountaineer colors hanging from the blackboard and from the ceiling down to my desk. I couldn't believe my eyes.

Even the boys and everybody had known about this surprise party. Jerry McHenry lit the candles and everybody crowded around and sang "Happy Birthday to You." They yelled that I should make a wish. Well, I did make a wish. And I got all the candles in one breath. Then Mrs. Porter started cutting the cake and everybody got quiet. I didn't understand why they would be so quiet. Even Herby and Piper and all the boys.

But then Susannah and Shadean went in the coatroom and came out with a box with a great big bright green ribbon around it. The Mountaineers' color again, but I didn't think about it at that moment.

A birthday card on top of the box had everybody's name signed inside. Then I really got embarrassed, and I wished I didn't have to open the present.

But I did open it, and oh, I was so happy I almost cried, well, actually I did cry a little bit, in the box was a Spalding left-handed first baseman's glove of cowhide, with leather laces. My very own. My very own glove to use on May 28. It was so startling to have such a present from everybody in grade six, I hardly knew what to say, but I said, "Thank you, everybody," and they all laughed. Herby jumped up and started to show me how to adjust the strap, but I already knew.

I began pounding my fist in that beautiful new glove right away, to break it in by May 28.

But I had to miss practice because of picking up brush from the pruning of the fruit trees. Well, everybody else in our family was doing it too. It took only a few days, and then I was back at practice again.

The worst part was when I was picking up brush near the new pear trees I found four of them dead, and my brother found six more. The deer tracks in the mud were a clear clue. My dad was so mad, but a deer fence between the woods and the orchard has to be at least eight feet high so the deer can't leap over it, and we didn't even have the money to buy the wire fencing. My father worried and wondered what to do. Shig added up what a fence would cost, and it was just too much.

Peggy and I were tied for winner of the school spelling bee, and one of us was going to go down to River Bend the next week after the Bat to compete against the 6th graders from the other schools. While we ran around the bases at recess, Ellen and Susannah and some others shouted words to us and we had to spell them. "Franchise!" "Galaxy!" "Occupation!" "Electoral!" "Opportunity!" "Migration!" "Immigration!" We had to spell them very fast, between one base and the next. Sometimes it was very silly when I would get almost to the bag with a whole bunch of letters to go. I wanted it to be Peggy who went to the county bee because I'd be so embarrassed in front of all those people.

Forgetting how to speak Japanese wasn't working. I couldn't unlearn what I had known. At school of course I never spoke any. None of us four Nisei did. When I walked out of the house in the morning to get on the school bus, I was all American for the whole day. Then when I got off the bus in the afternoon, I was Japanese again. It was so hard to unlearn words I had said all my life.

When I was with my friends it was easier. I often spent the night at Peggy's, and never thought in Japanese while I was there. Peggy has her very own sheep which she has raised, and it got to know me. At night Peggy and I brushed each other's hair in front of her mirror. She said she wished her hair wasn't so bendy and boring brown, she said mine is much nicer. I don't know if she meant it or if she was just being nice.

You can't always tell 100 percent with *hakujin,* if they are saying the truth or not. I tried to forget that word and thousands of others. I kept thinking there would be some way to make it work.

Some kids in our class were able to unlearn things. Donald might not remember from Friday to Monday about moving the decimal point, and Vernell could forget a word or a fact overnight.

And I couldn't forget simple things like *hashi,* chopsticks, or *ayatori,* cat's cradle. I tried to think that cat's cradle had no other name but cat's cradle. But it didn't work.

And I couldn't change my eyes. They are my eyes.

Even with all the mess of our house and the deer eating our pear trees, and even being the only Japanese in our grade, I was so happy to be back in Bear Creek Ridge. I had so many good things here. And in spring when the cherry trees came into bloom again, it was as if they were wearing enormous white dresses. I would sit in the swing, which Shig and I raised higher off the ground, and pump myself up in the air. I would empty out my mind and swing. Like a little kid. There was no panda anymore, but the swing was still there, and I was in it.

Manzanita and Shazam

Manzanita, left field

I refused to believe what they were saying about how Shazam's mother Floy was not even married when she got Shazam inside her. They said her and a boy did it and she got in the family way and she had to go away.

I flat refused to go along with it.

I decided to think about the things I knew for positive were true. It was when I had to hoe the ground for the garden I did the thinking. My mom did not want Darlene's mom to get ahead of her on tomatoes. They try to beat each other every year.

I knew I could be depended on to play my part on the team. There were those that didn't think so. They thought God would put the spirit in me when I was supposed to be fielding, they didn't know how God is at all.

God wants me to do my best every day in everything I

do, so why in heaven's name would He put the spirit in me when I was supposed to be doing my job, I ask you? Coach Rayfield kept telling us all the time how we had to "take good care of the ball." God wouldn't want me not to take good care of the ball if I was anywhere near it, would He?

Well, I didn't let it bother me none. God lets everybody know what their job is, I knew I could depend on Him always and forever into eternity, Amen. I fielded very good, Coach said I had good judgment also. So how could I have bad judgment on game day? I hoed the garden breaking up the dirt for the vegetables and I knew I could just go on leaning on His everlasting arms.

When Alva got her fielder's glove in her Easter basket just exactly the glove she wanted, it was clear proof of God. The glove was Wilson genuine cowhide with a perfect pocket for catching. She earned the whole $6.75 herself, working chores for the third-grade teacher that got her leg broke. Alva took her new glove to Sunday School on Easter, she was breaking it in already.

So we all had our gloves, even Shazam, due to Coach's daughter Dotty sending her one from the sports department at the state college. Dotty was all set to be our first-base coach and she sent Shazam the glove in the mail, it was her pleasure she said.

We knew we was lucky to have Dotty Rayfield come up from the college to be our first-base coach, she was MVP in her year, 1940. She come up already twice, at Christmas and her spring vacation. She made us learn her signals whether to go on or stay on first, and we did drills to remember them.

My dad mended the backstop, and him and Hallie's dad and some fathers from up on the Ridge made new bleacher benches for three that was split. And Ila Mae's dad brought his tractor and mower and he cut the grass around the edge of the field so our home field would be neat looking.

And I had only 1 hole in my face from scratching at a chicken pock. A very small hole. I did not have the self-control I should of had.

Those were my thoughts in the hoeing. And setting out the tomatoes and planting the peas and spinach also. The dirt was even warming up. We was running along the road quite regular to build up our endurance, and we only had to have indoor practices 4 times on account of rain.

When Shazam found out we would get to wear white shirts with red numbers sewed on the back, and our red shorts, she chose the number 7, and she bragged on how her grandmother would sew her number on. Most of us wanted to sew our own but there was no rule about we had to. I knew Shazam would not have the patience with the needle and thread when it knotted up on her, so it was better her grandmother was doing it.

We had so many flowers starting. It was like they say a new beginning when Jesus rose on Easter, and the earth had growing things popping out of it in blessed springtime.

Shazam, center field

I always put my puka-shell necklace on top the red silk scarf every different place I live. Little tiny white shells just the way they was when my dead father give me the necklace he was still alive he didnt know he would be dead in the bottom of the sea. He give me the scarf and puka-shell necklace in Hawaii my birthday I turned 3 I never seen him no more. In these shells there was animals but there isnt no more. They are famous Hawaii shells. There is palm trees in a picture on the silk.

I dont have my gas mask they took it away.

The necklace is full grown jewelry not for a little kid I save it every time. I always keep it wrapped in the Hawaii scarf when I am leaving to go live another place. When I get to the new place I unwrap it I put it on a special spot I have it on the apple box at Grammamas house here at Barlow.

I do not never wear it they might get hurt.

I come on the Greyhound to live with Grammama so my mom can get on her feet.

I bring that necklace and that scarf every place I live.

My mom she hit me I forgot the gas mask I said I forgot she said dont dare forget them Japs bomb us again you die without no gas mask I wont have nobody. It hurt when she hitted. I always tried to remember the gas mask hang the bag on my shoulder all the time over to the sugarcane fields the beach too where puka shells growed on the beach.

Over to Idaho them little children messed with my puka shells. I popped them in the face my mom went to hit me I outran her.

Nobody never give me no say so. Everybody putted me in places made me stay there. I never got to say where I live.

Over here to Grammamas it is OK. There is the fire dream but that is everywhere. The fire dream too loud I cant hear with the noise.

Too many bombs on my only fathers ship I cant remember how to do 7 X 7 Audrey she said sure you can Shazam Wink said it too. The fire dream in the night the 7 times in the day it pushed too loud on me I couldnt.

Mrs Winters said we are all learning these timeses everybody in this room. I did try then those bad bombers come in my head my mom crying.

Hallie was my friend she made me go to her place play ball with her and her dad. No fire no bombs when I play ball. Her mom made cookies she give me a sack full for my grammama I give her when I got home.

In Hallies house there was water running in the sink in a faucet I could not see no pump. They have their toilet in the house.

Hallies father hit us fungoes back of their woodshed I fielded better than Hallie on 3 of them. More than that but I lost count. Hallie has her own bedroom with her mom made her a cover to put on top her bed with zigzag stripes of red and blue on the white.

Her own father made a table beside her bed. He made it out of wood. It is her own table. If I had a father.

They have a plaster bear paw print in their front room a foot of a real bear that walked in their woods. It sets by the radio.

They had a Jap man over there to Hallies house. Nobody told me how come they had him over there I was going to home in Mr. Hallies pickup when I seen him.

You never know one could sneak up. I dont have my gas mask they took it away said we dont need it maybe we do you never know.

I told Hallies father in his pickup he could get that Jap good over to his house. He said Huh what did you say I said you could get him good that Jap over there. He said Shirley they are our neighbors. He should call me Shazam my name. We went on home.

No gas masks at Hallies house. Maybe in the closet. I did not see none.

My own father give me my name. Shazam there she is he said. I jump into his arms my mom told me many times how he said Shazam there she is and he would make like to let me fall then he would catch me and he would laugh. I seen my mom laugh when she told me.

Them Halloween trick or treaters over to Idaho my mom

said Go way you Jap faces she slammed the door. They did not get no candy. Get away from here you Japs she told them she did not give them none of our candy. She give it to the others that had plain eyes.

They was Jap children in costumes of a witch and a cat and a ghost. They ran around the side of the porch they never come back there.

Them Japs they made you a orphan. She explained me the Japs over and over again so I never forget. The bombs on my fathers ship all the fire all around. We did not have our gas masks anymore in Idaho. Here either.

That bed was so crowded with little ones that wet their-self when we lived over to Idaho I did not like to sleep with those several children. It was in the trailer house I thought we was going on trips with that man my mom said the war was over we would see the country but we never went on one single trip. The trailer stayed where it was the whole time. The wheels was gone from it. Too many little children they left their Tinkertoys all over the floor they got sand in the bed too. And that one window leaked.

Then I come over to Barlow to live with Grammama to have a bed by myself by the stove it is warm all the night. When the fire dream come.

The snow got deep I did not know snow got so deep. She made me clean my plate at suppertime she makes pot roast so good I cleaned my plate without her saying so.

She has napkins for our laps she makes me fold mine every time.

She sewed me a dress. 2 dresses. And then some blouses. On the sewing machine she has.

From the first day I got to this place it wasn't like the other places we been my mom and me. There is a game Bat 6. I could pitch just as good as Ila Mae but Coach made me go to center field he said Im important there.

In the kitchen by the pump there is a mirrow on the wall where I put on my red Pioneers cap. I looked in the mirrow I said Center field for the Pioneer team. My grammama sewing my number 7 on a white blouse on the back.

There was water in the faucet at Winks house too I went to the party I won the prize I took it home let it set on the crate besides my bed. When my grammama tucked me up in the night she always shook the snow globe and the snow fell down on the little people every time.

I told Grammama I dont need no tucking up Im big. She said any child sleeps better they get tucked up at night, I do not know. I still get the fire dream. Some nights not every night. It comes if somebody tucks me up or not. My mom did not tuck me up and I slept good. But the fire dream when it come I dont sleep good. When we lived with those children of that man I forget his name in the trailer I did not sleep good there. Me and my mom left that trailer house and I come over here to Barlow.

My grammama kissed me good night in the nighttime every since I come here. One night when the fire dream come I woke up in the dark she was kissing me on my hair. I said how come and she said I was crying in my sleep.

My mom said dont think about the fire dream itll go away and my grammama kissed me on the hair. It is the same either way.

Grammama is a spooky old lady that gets headaches.

I could of been a good shepherd in the play at the church it was about a doll in a barn. I had me a shepherd stick and shepherd robe and a shepherd cloth around my head. But they had a Jap shepherd too that Jap face made me dizzy I left.

How come my mom sent me here where they have Japs. And no gas masks. I did not ask her she was crying so bad.

Alva got her glove in a Easter basket she worked for the money to buy it and it come in her basket with the eggs.

Dotty Rayfield down to the college got me a glove. The ones in the sports box was too tore to use. The glove come in a package to school. And Coach Rayfield let me have a bat and ball too from the sports box for home. I went out back the chicken coop I hit fungoes there I can hit that tree. My job was dig potatoes and feed the chickens I hit fungoes after. I tagged the chickens out at the bases which are stumps Grammama says dont you do that you get them hysteric. I did it sometimes not all the time.

My job was shovel snow when it come down a lot also. It like to broke my back shoveling.

And bring in wood for the stove.

The Japs killed my only father I ever had. They bombed him in his ship the *Arizona* down at the Pearl Harbor I was too little to get a chance to have a father. If he was alive my mom would be on her feet.

My mom said he did too get married to her. She showed me the picture of them together they must of got married.

I hit so many home runs against the boys I was the best one. Some boys said they would not play no more but Kayo Riley he always played. They brought the sister of Hallie after school to strike me out one day. I got hits off of her too.

The snow melted and grass come up Grammama had yellow flowers by the porch. We had to make a mothers day card in school when we was done we had to go to the 2nd grade room help them do cards too. Theirs was messier than mine.

I made mine with blue color for Grammama. We was supposed to write words in the card Brita Mae wrote many words inside her card to her mom. And Alva too. Kayo Riley made a picture that come up off the page if you pulled on it then it sprung back he let me pull it. I did not write words but I put my name in big letters.

Mrs Winters said I know all your mothers so happy these pretty cards on mothers day. I got so bad feelings I did not tell nobody it made me so mad that stomach squeeze. I did not make my mom a card she come here for Christmas brang me that green dress I worn to Winks party but my mom cried all the time how bad her poor life was. I went away out behind the chicken coop in the snow I hit fungoes to the tree. I did not listen to my mom cry all the time Grammama she listened she made her arms go around my mom all the time. I had 2 fire dreams then.

I made my card for my grammama.

Snow melted we got outside practice I always caught flies good and grounders too. I can move over to right when a batter hits over there I can move left too when the ball comes that way. I threw to the right base every time. Coach hollered You throw to the wrong base you could lose us the game he did not mean me.

Coach said I was relief pitcher.

We all got our red numbers sewed on our blouses. My grammama finished mine there was 4 more days to the Bat game and there going to be hot dogs there from the Boy Scouts Brita Marie promised.

I never played a game with uniforms and hot dogs and the Star Spangled. My grammama said sure she would go to the game she hardly never went noplace Darlenes dad promised take us my grammama ironed her dress to wear and she had a hat for the sun. I had my red Pioneer cap setting on the apple box with my puka beads. Not on top of them nothing goes on top of them. At the side. Alongside the snow globe shaker thing from Winks party I won there.

The night before the game Grammama made merang cookies. She made me take my turn to beat up the egg whites her arm got tired. The cookies was to take to the church ladies booth along with doilies she already made they was in a box. I said how come. I thought it was a game of sports. She said it is that and other things people selling things for the church too she said it is a good time for everybody. She does not go to the church she made doilies for the booth. She said it was neighborly. Then the fire dream come I couldnt breathe and then morning come. I put on my red shorts and my number 7 blouse and my red Pioneer cap for the game. Grammama cooked me up flapjacks and sirup she said she was proud to go to the game see me play so good for the Pioneer team.

THE FIFTIETH ANNIVERSARY BAT 6
MAY 28, 1949
BARLOW ROAD GRADE SCHOOL PLAYING FIELD
BATTING ORDER

BEAR CREEK
RIDGE   BARLOW

Tootie   **Hallie**
Kate   **Ila Mae**
Shadean   **Wink**
Aki   **Darlene**
Lorelei   **Shazam**
Ellen   **Audrey**
Daisy   **Alva**
Little Peggy   **Brita Marie**
Susannah   **Manzanita**

Vernell, manager and general sub

The Boy Scouts were the first ones to get to the ball field to set up their weenie roast and build the fire. We got there plenty early too, my dad was one of the dads helping take up the tarpaulins they laid down the night before on account of somebody thought it would rain and they were right. Just an itty bit of rain in the night and bright and clear blue on the Bat 6 morning. Seven dads picked up the tarps together, some I did not know from Barlow.

My mom's old cousin that sits in McHenrys' Store at the woodstove came early in a car too with the retired Bluc brothers, one of them with his harmonica for "Oh, Say, Can You See." My mom joked how they like to get there early to criticize the way the Boy Scouts build their weenie-roast fire.

My mom carried her pies in a box with a towel over the top of the box so not to get dust on them, there was 29 pies in the church ladies' booth. And the Gospel Church ladies had preserves and cookies and jam and crocheted doilies and what-all over in their booth. I went over there with my mom and she said hi to those ladies she knows from working in the fruit packing house. Their booth had red and white crepe-paper streamers for the Barlow team.

Old Louella got brought to the game early too, like always. She took her embroidered dish towels she had sewed over to the Poor Fund booth, for them to sell and get money for the poor people, she does not believe in churches. It took her a long time to walk over there and back on account of her cane. Then she set down to watch the players warming up.

She gazed at the batting order that Mr. Porter gave into her hands, she had her green sun visor on her head and she read up and down the list in the visor shadow.

Where she was sitting was her rocking chair they put on the quilt they laid out on her spot behind the third-base line, and she had a apple box there with her Thermos bottle of tea and her bottle of aspirins too sitting on it.

I heard her say, "Gals gonna catch their death, those short pants. Them breezes from down to the crick. That there's a smart one, that tall stick of a gal. . . ." There was one Barlow girl in long slacks, I hardly ever saw such a tall girl. Not in grade school.

Mr. Porter made me throw and catch with Lorelei and Susannah till he said I could stop and go to the bench where I wanted to be, guarding our bats and the water can.

Herby left his old black and white and yellow dog with me so he could work at the weenie-roast fire. He tied the leash around one leg of our bench. I did not want the dog there, my mind wanders and I had to concentrate on keeping the bats and the water and the towels as neat as a pin. But Herby just attached the dog there and said See you later Vernell and he went away. He thinks he's so big being 12 and starting to be a Boy Scout.

Nobody told me I would have to have a dog too, along with everything else. I told the dog to lay down and behave himself. Then I felt bad from the look on his face and I petted him and he laid down besides one of my legs, my left one I guess.

Kate, second base

The excitement was almost too much to take sitting down, like we all agreed. Daisy woke up with a kink in her throwing arm, but her mom rubbed linament on it. Daisy kind of smelled from it, but her arm was better. We got to have batting warmup first, on account of being the visiting team.

We pretended we weren't nervous. All except Susannah, who admitted she was very nervous. Vernell too, but she had the bats, balls, towels, and water all lined up by the time I got to the field. Her mom and dad brought two milk cans full of water in their pickup. She had the ladle all laid out for us, she had done a excellent job.

Well, the Barlow team had some strong throwing and perfect catching and some missed balls just like our team. I could tell watching them warm up they would be hard to beat, and I got nervouser than I had thought I would be.

I watched the ambulance from River Bend drive over and park out near left field. They always have the ambulance there for an emergency that wouldn't hardly ever happen. My dad said the ambulance men just like to come and sit in the sun and watch the game.

Before the game there are many ceremonies. First, all the first graders from both schools march out on the field with their teachers and they make the Pledge of Allegiance and everybody stands at attention and says it with them. I remember when it was our turn in first grade to do this, it was on our home field and it seemed so important. Ellen wasn't with us then and neither was Aki. Now it's just a bunch of little kids with their hands over their hearts.

Then we had prayers by both preachers. We all bowed down our heads. Our minister said a prayer about peace for all time because like he said, "Those good ladies of 1899 found a way to stop the strife by playing sports with their hearts." He praised God for keeping "our special friend Louella" in good health to come to this year's ball game. And on account of Decoration Day he blessed the soul of her husband and her son, they both died in wars. Then he praised the coaches, he praised the Superintendent of Schools, he praised everybody's parents, he praised the sunshine. And he said to God, "Place your blessing on the girls that play this game today, may they bring courage and ladylike good sportsmanship to this playing field like has been done before, Amen."

And the Gospel minister from down at Barlow prayed a good prayer too: "We are all one family here in Your sight, oh Lord, even if we are different faiths, we are all gathered on the same playing field to bring glory to You with our annual game."

And after he asked God to bless the game, he said, "All you folks blessed by God to be here on this great day you all join me with a big Hallelujah!"

And we lifted up our heads from bowing, and we whooped. "Hallelujah!"

And he said, "Again, brothers and sisters!"

And we whooped "Hallelujah!" louder than before.

And he yelled. "One more time for the Lord!"

And everybody whooped again, very loud this time, "Hallelujah!"

It was very nice, but all I could think of was I had to hit a single or double, help get the bases loaded, and pray Aki would knock us all home.

Mrs. Porter said in our team huddle, "Remember, girls, we can't play ball with our teeth clenched. We get to have fun today. You've earned it. Go get 'em."

The "Star-Spangled Banner" was very excellent like the year before. It was the 3rd-grade teacher from Barlow with a violin and our principal's husband on clarinet plus one of the retired Blue brothers from McHenrys' Store porch with his harmonica. Everybody sang and it was then I realized how many, many people were there to watch us play. It was a loud song of our country, coming from many voices. I tried not to let so many onlookers disturb me.

Little Peggy, right field

While we were supposed to be lining up to do the tradition of shaking hands with the Barlow team, I was watching Mr. and Mrs. Porter standing with the Barlow coach and his wife, all laughing their heads off about something. I had been quite nervous about trying to play well, and I had woken up too early in the morning, full of worry. But seeing those coaches laughing and friendly, I was suddenly reminded it is just a game, it is not life and death who wins.

But because I had looked away at them I stepped into the wrong place in the lineup, and by accident I got between Aki and Lorelei. When I noticed my mistake and began to step out of line, we had to continue along shaking every hand, and Lorelei nudged me back into place ahead of her. So I ended up seeing something nobody else might have seen. It is because I am short and my head is lower to the ground, I suppose. Lorelei is much taller than me. She might not have looked down.

We were going along shaking hands and I saw a Barlow girl start to shake Aki's hand and then pull back like from a snake you might see in front of you. Then she fisted her hand against her stomach and moved along the line. She shook my hand and moved on to Lorelei.

Refused to shake Aki's hand.

I personally could not believe it.

I nudged Aki with my left hand while I was going on shaking with my right one. I said right up against her left ear, "I saw that. I'm gonna say something —" And Aki shook her head and said it was okay, it didn't matter.

I personally had a disagreement with Aki, it did matter. I whispered very hissingly in her ear, "It does too matter, that isn't good sportsmanship." Aki just shook her head again with no expression at all on her face and got in line to sing "Oh, Say, Can You See."

The minute the song was done, old Louella said in her old squeaky voice, "Play ball!" And the people in the bleachers and standing all around the ball field clapped their hands.

The Superintendent of Schools threw out the ball to the Barlow pitcher and I went over to our bench, behind third base.

Shadean, pitcher

I picked up my favorite Spalding from the row of bats Vernell had laid out, saying to myself, This is the only time of my life I might ever play such an important game in front of so many people. I kept saying to myself, This is the real game.

Seeing Piper's dad in his umpire's uniform again from last year when he had umpired so good on our home field made me feel easier. Having a son in our class made him closer to us. Not that he would favor us, I don't mean that. It just made the game feel familiar. He said, "Play ball!" and the game we had waited our whole lives to play was upon us.

Our batting order was a good one. We all had confidences in Tootie, she is a very good hitter, she just had to have good pitches. Mr. Porter always told Tootie to wait till she saw a pitch she liked.

Mr. and Mrs. Porter were where they told us they would be, we could count on Mrs. Porter for first-base coach and Mr. Porter at third. Even if he did have to do all the signals with one hand.

Their pitcher was very concentrated. She checked her infielders before every pitch, she looked hard at the catcher, she had a windup you couldn't tell exactly when she was going to release the ball. And her name kept getting shouted over and over again from the audience: "Okay, Ila Mae, okay, Ila Mae!"

Tootie waited through three pitches she didn't like. One was called a strike and two were balls, and then she sent a grounder way out to right field, and she hollered, "See you later!" and ran. It almost looked liked a foul but it wasn't, and their right fielder stopped it backhand. A very good scoop, she looked like she had practiced that a lot. But Tootie made it to second easy, and she stayed there very confident, shaking out her wrists and waiting. Their second baseman I had seen at the Barlow General Store. She wouldn't let Tootie get very far around second, she followed her with her body. Their right fielder had very beautiful hair, all hanging down from the back of her cap.

I heard people on the bleachers shouting things: "Beautiful Hair, Beautiful Hair," and "Okay, Ila Mae, okay, Ila Mae," and "Rootie Tootie, Rootie Tootie, Rootie Tootie!" all at once. I looked around and it looked pretty as a picture, parents and grandmoms and dogs and babies and the hot-dog roasting fire and the booths full of pies and plates of fudge. I thought, Yes sir, this is the real thing.

Kate was up next. Tootie hollered at her from second, "Hubba hubba, Kate!" Kate needs a good pitch too, but she will swing at more different kinds than Tootie will, she had one strike called on her too, it was way low but Piper's father is a fair umpire and only some little kids booed the call. And someone was hollering, "Make her pitch to you, Kate!" Then the next ball that came Kate swung and it went to their shortstop who threw it to first, and Kate was out but Tootie had gotten to third.

In the bleachers they were hollering, "Yea, Alva, yea, Wink, yea, Barlow!"

I stepped up to bat.

For a moment I just listened to the sound of my name being yelled from the bleachers. I think I will always remember that feeling.

I tapped my bat on the plate and concentrated. We had Tootie on third base and 1 out. I had to get on base myself, knock Tootie home, and let Aki come up to drive me in. Those Barlow girls had good fielding out there. I could feel their catcher behind me being alert, kicking the dirt, taking charge. In the bleachers there was my name being yelled. And my mom and dad were back there behind me. I heard their voices.

I got a good, hard pitch at the start. I swung.

And I was too late. It landed in the catcher's mitt and she threw it back out to the pitcher.

"Eyes open, Shadean," I could hear Mr. Porter from over near third, and I also heard the Barlow coach hollering, "On your toes, Darlene."

I socked a hard grounder on the very next pitch. The loud swat of the wood felt beautiful, and I got safe to first base because the Barlow shortstop overthrew the ball, it ricocheted right off the huge giant first baseman's glove. But then such a surprise happened, that first baseman being so tall in her legs, she fetched it from foul territory in time to throw it home and put Tootie out. Tootie had waited at third to see what would happen, then she ran home on the overthrow, and the catcher tagged her. It was fair and square and awful.

Poor Tootie and poor Kate, I was thinking.

I was on first with 2 outs, and it was up to Aki.

"Yea, Shadean!" came from the bleachers. "Good job, Shadean" came from Mrs. Porter at first base. Ka-boom, ka-boom came from inside me, where I was excited, nervous, and relieved. Their first baseman standing over me was so tall, taller than Mrs. Porter standing there.

And then came Aki, our cleanup man. "Aki! Aki! Aki!" the people were shouting. And Tootie on the bench, hollering "Hubba hubba ding ding" to cheer her on. My brain was so excited. I was leaning off first. Aki circled her bat in the air a little bit, the way she always did, getting ready. Their pitcher gave her a low one that Aki didn't like and she let it pass by. Again, voices from the bleachers, "Ah-kee, Ah-kee!"

I was tempted to steal second, I looked in Mrs. Porter's face right near me. She was holding me back by holding her breath. "Watch her, Wink!" somebody shouted.

The next pitch was a low, slow one and that one passed by too. Two balls. My legs were so ready to steal. Then came Aki's pitch, chest level and smooth. She swung at it and I ran to second, Mr. Porter signaled me to come on to third, I ran toward him, and he was looking out past me with his hand just raised but not moving, and I got close to third and his hand went into motion telling me to go on home, and my foot pounded the corner of the bag and I kept running.

I scored.

And then in came Aki, and the bleachers were jumping up and down with voices. Aki and me hugged each other and Ellen and Daisy and Tootie who were there hugged us too.

All I knew was that ball had gone out there somewhere toward center field. I didn't hear it explained till later.

2–0.

Everyone was yelling so loud, it must have been hard for Lorelei to make sense, but there she was at the plate, and I had to hope this was a good day for her which she sometimes does not have.

And she didn't. Ila Mae got Lorelei out but it took her seven pitches to do it because Lorelei hit two foul balls before striking out. I have to hand it to Lorelei, she was determined.

I was so proud of myself. I knew it was not nice to be cocky. I couldn't help it.

Naturally, Aki wasn't proud of herself, she never is. But she was excited and grinning ear to ear like me.

And then I found out how come it happened. Barlow's phenomenon player totally fumbled the fly Aki hit. It rolled around out there in center field till their left fielder got it and by then it was too late, we'd scored 2 runs.

Not much of a phenomenon ball player. I would never want to miss a fly and let 2 runs come in.

Daisy, third base

I saw it happen. Aki's fly wasn't that hard to catch. A good fielder could of caught it. Barlow's center fielder went toward it like a beginner, she fumbled it, it rolled away from her, and their left fielder had to pick it up and she couldn't get it all the way to home plate before our 2 runs came in.

It was so exciting for those runs to happen, but I could not help to watch out there in the outfield, how bad of a error that was.

We had heard this girl was a phenomenon player.

Then she just stood there.

If we went on playing this good, and if that phenomenon went on fumbling flies, we had such a good chance of winning, I was almost too nervous to remember to pick up my glove from the bench before heading on out to third base. I saw my dad up there in the bleachers and I thought about him talking to Lorelei's dad if we won. I wanted to be able to see into the future and yet I did not want to.

Aki, first base

I would not think that fly I hit could take both Shadean and me around the bases. But it did, and the girls jumped up and down and we hugged. Up in the bleachers people were congratulating my dad and mom and I was so glad we had come back to the Ridge where everything had begun to go so right.

Brita Marie, second base

Coach Rayfield didn't go out to third base right away. Dotty Rayfield went over to coach at first, but Coach stayed at the bench. We girls were trying to think of all the right things at once, like concentrate, don't get nervous, breathe deep, take good care of the ball, always know where the runners are, do good for your school, keep your team spirit, and besides that we were all out of balance by being down 2–0 in the first inning.

And it was Shazam that did it to us.

I had never seen her fumble a ball so bad.

She was way over on the end of the bench with that look in her face and Coach Rayfield was over there with her. I wanted to listen but I knew we were not supposed to. I just paced back and forth on the ground. Being 8th in the batting order I had much time to wait.

I looked up there where Darlene's mom was sitting with Shazam's old grandmother. Darlene's mom was alert to the game, the old lady was not. She kept moving her hat around to keep the sun out of her eyes.

The first 3 batters were Hallie, Ila Mae, and Wink. Wink was the only one wearing long pants, the rest of us had our red Barlow shorts on. Sliding is very important to Wink's life. She really worships that Hank Greenberg and she wants to be a big league player, even though how would anybody find her here in Barlow and take her away to the big leagues of Detroit? And besides she is a girl and everything.

Wink, first base

I could not help thinking about the catastrophe error Shazam made in center field.

And then she was over on the end of our team bench with Coach Rayfield talking down real close to her and her keeping that look on her face with her mouth bent, and not looking back at him in the eye.

And I could not help thinking how my mom said how Floy never did get married to anybody. I wished she didn't say that.

I picked up my bat and swung it in the air. Shazam could go loony on us but we could still win. Hank Greenberg would want me to keep my mind on the game very good.

Audrey, catcher

2-nothing! And for the reason of Shazam fumbling that ball like a child.

I had paid attention very good, and I gave signals very good to Ila Mae. That pitch she pitched to that 4th hitter was a hard pitch to connect with for a average player. But that Japanese girl was not any average player. She had good batting judgment and I had a moment of wishing she was on our team.

How could Shazam fumble the ball like that? I had to admit it beat me.

And then she went over to the bench and stayed there with her arms stuck to her body, you couldn't talk to her. I wouldn't know what to say anyway. I never heard nobody say to Shazam, "How come you fumbled the ball?" for the simple reason she never did so before.

Hallie, right field

I was first in the batting order. I was wearing my sister's winning socks from the 1945 Bat 6, she gave me them that morning by surprise, she saved them all those years and there they was on the table beside my orange juice at breakfast. My whole family knew but me till that minute when I saw them. I was grateful like anybody would be and I put them on before I ate my eggs.

There I was in those socks, and my mom and dad sitting

behind the backstop were cheering for me. And my sister was over there working the scoreboard, putting the numbers in the holes, it was her privilege for being MVP in her year of 1945. I felt scrunched, seeing she had put up the big wooden 2 in the visiting-team spot and we still had that big staring zero.

I chose my favorite bat and I swung a few warmup swings, I took a drink of water from the water cup Lola and Lila had set on a card table beside our bench. I saw Lola had her grumpy look on her face, she saw Shazam fumble that ball and Lola could of fumbled it just as good herself. I gave Lola a look in sympathy but I could not stop and make any more over it than that. I went to the plate knowing I could make Barlow proud of me.

There were many voices hollering, "Beautiful Hair! Beautiful Hair!" This is a name I wish I never had, it's such a embarrassment.

But there was no third-base coach out there, and Dotty Rayfield and the umpire said we was going to wait a few minutes for him to get there. Coach Rayfield was still on our bench with Shazam. His head and hands were moving, she was still as a stone.

We waited and waited. The umpire said, "It'll be a couple of minutes, folks," and he said the Ridgers could keep warming up out there. Their pitcher and catcher threw the ball to each other, then to the different bases. I swung my bat some more times.

Dotty Rayfield had her hands on her hips, waiting.

The two umpires stood and waited too. The base umpire, Brita Marie's uncle, paced a little bit back and forth out there in the dirt.

Then some people in the bleachers started singing "Take Me Out to the Ball Game."

Manzanita, left field

I think Coach Rayfield was trying to find out what got into Shazam. I was thinking it was a good thing the Lord was watching over my fielding talent. You couldn't just leave a ball roll around out there in center field till kingdom come. I did my best and they still scored 2 runs, I felt so bad.

Coach Rayfield kept everybody waiting while he sat with Shazam. It didn't seem like it was fair. Well, not exactly not fair neither. He was a coach of everybody and that included cuckoo Shazam. And with all the surprise of her missing that out, Coach was just doing his job. It was his job to jolly us back to good spirits like he done many a time with we girls. He had done it with Lola and Lila, he had done it with Audrey, he did it with me in the mud last fall when I got downhearted just because my hands was so cold they felt like falling off.

Shazam, center field

Too many Jap faces everywhere. I couldnt breathe. Them Jap eyes in the bleachers and over by the Boy Scout cookfire.

That one on the Ridge team with them slanty eyes in her face she stood there wobbling her bat I couldnt breathe.

Sneaky Japs never warned nobody they snuck behind our backs dropped bombs right in my fathers ship the *Arizona* he was down in it without no warning.

Coach Rayfield he comes over to me on the bench he says Shazam you had a unlucky moment out there but we can recover. He looks at me in my face. You feeling okay Shazam he says.

Ila Mae told me way back then I wouldnt get to play the famous Bat game if I said that word I kept my mouth shut tight not to let it come out.

Shazam Coach says again. You want me to send Lola out to center for you next inning he says.

No I tell him to make him go away.

But he dont go away. He sits there. Then he tells me You can knock that ball real hard and make us proud. I know you can do it Shazam.

I dont say nothing.

You remember your batting order he says in my face.

I tell him yeah Im after Darlene.

He says Good girl Shazam you can get them Ridgers. He

puts his hand on my knee and he stands up and goes back out to third where he coaches.

Too many Japs that killed my father down under the water in the ship.

Alva, shortstop

I said this prayer just before our half of the inning. I did not know what was going on or I would of prayed so different.

Dear God,

Thank You God for the admireful way Ila Mae pitched this whole time, with the ball in excellent control.

I do not understand Your ways of working, for Shazam dropped that fly she should not drop. Was I supposed to back her up out there in center field? If I had been there, would I make any difference?

Thank You for my catch of that girl with the long hair's ball. I threw it good to Wink, didn't I? But the overthrow I am sorry about. It ended up good but I apologize anyway.

Thy will be done.

Your friend,

Alva

Ila Mae, pitcher

Well, Coach went back over to third, and their pitcher gets lined up and everybody's ready to go. The spectators stopped singing "Take Me Out to the Ball Game," which they sung almost 3 times. Hallie steps to the plate and I kind of held my breath. Not for any real reason, maybe, but I begun to be a little edgy. Bright sunshine and our big day and the smoky smell of hot dogs cooking over there, but just some slight jittery feeling come over me.

That Ridge pitcher has a different kind of windup, it is a kind of figure 8, she pitched 3 in a row I would strike at but Hallie waited.

And when she swung she hit it real nice, out to center where I had seen her hit it so many times before, she actually made it look easy, and she was off running and Dotty Rayfield signaled her to go on past first. Their center field had threw the ball but it wasn't even close yet, their redhead second base was leaning off her base to catch it, and Hallie stomped on the bag and stayed.

"Yea, Beautiful Hair! Beautiful Hair! Barlow, go Barlow!" was coming out onto the field from behind me.

I was up. I did not know before I would be so jittery with excitement.

Man, their pitcher knew what she was doing. She stared into the strike zone and she almost put a kind of bend on the ball, I let 2 of them go by before I settled down. I thought it might of been a mistake on account of I probably could of hit them, the ump called one a ball and one a strike and I was actually of the same opinion.

But guess what Hallie did, she stole third just as pretty as you please.

"Beautiful Hair! Beautiful Hair! Beautiful Hair! All the way, Ila Mae! Ila Mae! Ila Mae! Ila Mae! Barlow, yea! Yea, Barlow!"

It sounded so good.

I remembered my brief wish from long ago that I would be MVP for our year. I knew it was selfish. And yet it come back to me, standing there with the pitch coming, and I swung the bat.

Wheek! I felt like an airplane, I took off so fast, and I knew the ball was somewhere out there kind of low, I watched Dotty Rayfield's hands tell me not to try to go to second, and I crossed the first base good and safe.

And Hallie scored. I had hit the ball deep into center field and their center fielder threw to their shortstop but Hallie just went parading right on home. I was so proud.

Dotty Rayfield was telling me "Good job, Ila Mae" and the Ridge first baseman gave me room and I was getting settled with my foot on the bag and some little picture in my mind kept coming in and going out while I was watching Wink step to the plate. The Ridge pitcher and first baseman had their eyes on each other and they were both concentrating on me. It felt a little bit scoonchy but it was exciting, too. My breathing felt so loud.

Wink standing there at bat was a sight for eyes to see. She is so tall, 5 feet and 10 inches, she makes a impression wherever she is, and with her Pioneer cap and that Hank Greenberg jersey and her red slacks, anybody could see this was a girl that come here to play ball.

Like I did, Wink held her fire while she got used to that pitcher. I was like a rubber band ready to ping.

Darlene was taking warmup swings, and Coach Rayfield did a very unexpected thing, he walked away from third again and he goes over to the bench and he got Shazam to stand up. I loosened my stance for a moment and I just watched, I kept my foot firm on the bag. Shazam went over to where Lola & Lila had the bats laid out and she picked up a bat and she walked around with it. Coach returned again to third.

Some odd little remembering came and went in my mind again. But I concentrated right through it.

Wink got her third pitch and she let that one go. Wink is a very smart ball player, she chooses good choices. Even so, she hit two foul balls, one of them went outside the first-base line their little short right fielder throws it back. Now the count is 2 and 2 and Wink swings.

Away I go! I had my eyes on the second-base bag and I run hard, and long before I cross the inside edge of it I hear Coach Rayfield over at third yelling at me, "Come on, Ila Mae!" and as I'm coming toward him his arm is windmilling around for me to go on home, and I do it, and I cross home plate and I have scored a run for my home team and I am bursting out of my shirt I am so proud.

"Yea, Ila Mae! Yea, Barlow! Yea, Ila Mae all the way!"

The bleachers are yelling on their feet and I intake my breath and look behind me. There's Wink, sliding the most pretty, dusty, skinny long-legged slide I ever saw her make, and the third basemen can't tag her out in time, Wink's foot is on that bag solid. Brita Marie's uncle is over there declaring she is safe, and Wink stands up, dusts off those red pants, kind of shakes out her long old legs, and stands up to her full heighth and waits for the action to start.

"Yea, Wink! Yea, Stringbean! Yea, Beanpole!"

The bleachers are all up and waving and shouting, and it is a blessful day and we are tied with the Ridge.

And the coaches: What a riot! They are congratulating each other! The man Ridge coach, the one with the arm partly missing, he's over there at their bench hollering to Coach Rayfield, "Your girls are good!" And Coach Rayfield is saying back to him, "Yours too!" And they're laughing like this is a picnic.

Wink, first base

I knew I was right to practice sliding all the time because look how good I slid. That third baseman would of tagged me if I didn't slide.

Hard work pays off they always say in my family and I was thinking how true it come for me. I was proud I had Hank Greenberg to inspire me.

Darlene was up next, and the crowd of onlookers yelled

for her, "Go, Darlene! Go, Darlene!" She hit a bouncing grounder to third and I couldn't go anywhere. But she beat the ball to first base easy, and there she stood, flexing her beefy legs, and we was all ready for the big moment. Shazam was up.

She steps to the plate and our team all chanted, "Sha-zam! Sha-zam! Sha-zam!" in good spirits for her to get a good hit which we knew she could do if she would concentrate which was never hard for her to do till this morning when she fumbled that fly. Shazam could bat both right and left, she was batting right that morning. Coach Rayfield joined in with our cheering and he signaled me to be ready to run. I was already ready, I was readier than I'd ever been. I had my hind foot on the bag and I was aiming myself toward home plate, hoping Shazam would be herself and knock me in, and Darlene would get around the bases too and

Shazam, center field

Too many Jap faces killed my only father I ever had.

Darlene, third base

Dotty Rayfield signaled me to be ready. The pitcher pitched the first pitch, Shazam swang and I ran.

Wink, first base

Shazam made contact. Smack. I was already in motion when Coach Rayfield said, "No, Wink!" I stopped sudden after 2 steps and went back to the bag. It was a sharp grounder, their 3rd baseman scooped it up and threw over to 2nd and Darlene was out. Then their redhead 2nd baseman threw to first for a double-play and I remember clear as day saying to myself: Drat. Phooey. Rats. If only I'd of known what was happening I would of said much worse.

Audrey, catcher

I will never know for sure if I did or didn't hear Shazam say any words before she swang or while she was swinging. They tried to get me to say I did or didn't but I could not say that.

Where I was, over there on deck, I saw the ball low in the air going from second to first and I was real disappointed for Shazam. She was going to be put out, I could see it coming.

But that feeling lasted only as long as a clock tick.

Hallie, right field

I wish I had never saw what I saw.

Brita Marie, second base

Why was Shazam running *inside* the baseline? She never did that before. Even way over there with Audrey on the other side of the plate, I could see Shazam's judgment was off. And then her brain went. Right in front of God and everybody, while the first baseman was still leaning out from the bag with the ball just landed in her glove from 2nd, Shazam turned her direction and her right elbow came up like an axe handle and cracked into the side of the girl's head so hard she went flat in the dirt.

Shazam *aimed* herself to do that.

It was impossible to think of doing such a thing.

Shazam did it.

Lola and Lila, managers

We saw it, we saw it all. We saw Shazam on purpose charge right toward the first baseman and bust her in the head with her elbow. We saw the first baseman go flat down on the ground, we saw everything. It was a crime to see in broad daylight.

Darlene, third base

By the time I turned around to see what had happened, Dotty Rayfield had gone over her legal line and was down on the dirt with the fallen first baseman.

And their little short right fielder was down there too, and then the Doc from up on the Ridge, and Coach Rayfield was running to first base and I saw what Audrey and Brita Marie was doing, and I near couldn't believe it all.

Brita Marie, second base

I did what I thought was best. I grabbed Audrey and we ran down the baseline and took ahold of Shazam where she was starting to walk away into foul territory, and we just held on to her.

Audrey, catcher

Even when Shazam begun to kick at us we didn't let go, we held on.

Ila Mae, pitcher

I get so furious raging mad every time I think of the sound that elbow made in that girl's bones.

Alva, shortstop

Dear God,
   How could this happen? Is it something I did?

11	**BEAR CREEK RIDGE GRADE SCHOOL**
AND	**BARLOW ROAD GRADE SCHOOL**

Kate, second base

When I saw Daisy's throw, all I wanted in the world was to make that out. And then all I wanted in the world was to make the double play. I threw as fast as I could to Aki, and the ball went more inside than I meant it to, and Aki had to lean in to get it, but she kept her foot on the bag like always, and she caught it perfect like always, and then her head jerked like it was shot and the next thing she was down on the ground and I could see the number 7 on the back of that Barlow girl's shirt as she was walking off into foul territory.

Shadean, pitcher

I did not move. Then I moved.

Susannah's father got there before me, he was on the ground saying Don't touch Aki, he was holding Little Peggy's arm where it was under Aki's neck, he was telling the arm, "Don't move a muscle."

I couldn't hear what he said to Aki.

Then everybody came in a swarm.

Little Peggy, right field

I put my arm under Aki's head which looked like I never saw her before, well, I put it under her neck really, and I wanted to know if she could hear me but Susannah's father took hold of my arm and said not to move a muscle. "Can you hear me, Aki?" he said, in his steady voice of a doctor.

Aki's eyes were closed. Her whole head looked so different.

I personally was stunned to see her so still, I will always remember that position of her face to my dying day. Susannah's father took off his jacket to put under Aki's neck and he made me take my arm out from under there, real slowly, even though I don't want to lose my touch of her body.

I never saw a face like that in my life. The swelling was getting huge.

Susannah's father felt with his hand under her ear and the Barlow first-base coach stood up to clear everybody away and get some peace and quiet.

Ila Mae, pitcher

What Coach Rayfield done he ran over from third to first base fast as his old middle-age legs would take him and he got down on the ground with that girl and he looked like he might be praying he was kneeling down so.

I would not blame him if he was.

Then so many people got there. It was Coach Rayfield and 3 other men that lifted that wounded first baseman on the stretcher into the ambulance.

Susannah, left field

Barlow's first-base coach went to the pitcher's box and put up her hands in the air for everybody to listen. She turned to every side and tried to hush everyone. Mr. Porter was helping her shush the people and get them orderly. Many little children were running around the field in confusion, and dogs were making such a racket.

While everybody was wondering what she would say, the River Bend ambulance drove very slow to first base. Men shooed the dogs away from the ambulance wheels. My stomach was sinking.

The first-base coach said, "There's been an accident, we don't know how bad yet. The Bear Creek Ridge first baseman has been injured. The doctor is with her, we'll just have to wait and see." And she and Mr. Porter said some words to each other I couldn't hear.

By that time that number 7 was in the clutches of the girls.

Ellen, shortstop

Susannah's mom and Little Peggy's mom had their arms around Aki's mom. The three of them came down out of the bleachers onto the field, and people moved aside so they could get through.

The thought went through my head, "There is the MVP for 1930, going to see her flesh-and-blood daughter hurt on the ball field."

The ambulance was at first base and 4 men were lifting Aki on a stretcher into the back door of it.

I only stood still.

Then Daisy and the big enormous tall Barlow girl walked over to Kate's base and I followed them. I did not know what else to do.

Wink, first base

Nobody had ever mentioned what we was supposed to do now. Not knowing any reason why not to go over to where the Ridgers' outfield was gathered together around second base, I did so, even shaking inside like I was. And Darlene come too, from over at second where she had been put out. The Ridgers were shy over there and Darlene and me was too. Brita Marie's uncle, the base umpire, had run over to first base.

I said my name to their third baseman. She said her name

to me, Daisy, and we looked in each other's eyes. Their center field said her name, Lorelei, and the rest of them. We all stood looking at each other.

I did not know what to say to them but I knew I had to say something on my own team's field. I said, "I'm real sorry what happened."

The third baseman that was hoping to tag me out just a few minutes before said, "It isn't your fault, Wink, you didn't do it."

She was right, it wasn't my fault. But I never saw such a thing before and it was too shocking to understand.

In despite of the ruckus going on, I looked down at my feet. When I sneaked a look I saw those other girls were all looking down at their feet too. I looked over at Darlene who was looking at me. I felt so bad looking at her, on account of we were on the same team with Shazam, we seen her every day, she won the prize at my birthday party by peeking under the blindfold. Darlene's face showed she felt horrible.

How was we supposed to be Christians now?

So many dogs were barking, they wouldn't stop.

Daisy, third base

Holy Mary, Mother of God, there was Aki in the ambulance.

Me and Ellen and the Barlow base runners all gathered together at second base, plus the outfielders. Some came slow, some came fast. I don't know why we went to second base.

Nobody said a word at first. Only surprised sounds with our breaths.

I looked over to where Mr. Porter was with Aki's father and her brother Shig. I couldn't imagine what they would be saying, there was so many sounds all around.

And the then big tall one, Wink, said she was sorry.

Mrs. Porter put her arms around Aki's mother who then climbed up in the ambulance and then it drove very slowly off the field.

If anybody was sorry it was me. I made the throw to second base. If I had thrown bad. Or if I had thrown late. Or if I hadn't scooped the grounder that number 7 hit. If something. That big tall Wink would have ran in, and maybe their next runner would too. Barlow might be ahead, but Aki would be standing up right now. I can't say words for how bad I felt.

What kind of insane person was that number 7, anyway?

Two trails of dust rose off the dirt behind the ambulance wheels.

Susannah said, "What's her name?"

Their big first baseman said, "Shazam."

Lorelei whispered it, like to get it straight, "Shazam." Then we were all silent with second base in the middle of us, and all that rowdiness going on in foul territory.

Vernell, manager

Some boys were yelling. "Get her! Get her good! She hit Aki!" And Herby's dog jumped so hard he broke the leash and went tearing off across the field making dust come up like a storm. He found some other dogs and joined their barking that could make you go deaf.

Hallie, right field

Right away when the first baseman went down, Darlene's mom attached herself to Shazam's old grandmother up there on the bleachers, and she kept holding her the whole time, even while everybody was upset and yelling and arguing she kept her arm around her. It was a terrible thing for that old lady. Having to see her own granddaughter do with her elbow like that. I would not ever in my life want my grandmother to see such a thing. But then it is different with me. I would not ever do such a thing.

Shazam's father died inside a bombed ship, and he never got to see her play ball. I remembered how Shazam walked out of the Christmas play down at the Gospel Church, and now this.

Audrey, catcher

With Coach Rayfield in the huddle at first base and Dotty Rayfield making the speech, the girls ourselves had took charge. Brita Marie had Shazam by her arm and held on, and Shazam tried to get away and I got her other arm and Shazam kicked, and by that time Lola was there so I give her my side and I got around under Shazam's armpits and held her in a tight hold from behind. Shazam was squirming and kicking everywhere, and us three Pioneer team girls held on for dear life in all that dust swirling.

Shazam didn't say anything while we was holding her, she just kicked and kicked and we held on. We didn't know anything else to do.

Lila, manager

Lola up and told me to mind the bench and sop up the mess of water spilled across everything when everybody jumped up. She leaped up and went to help hold on to Shazam over in foul territory. I just watched, I did not sop up any more of the water, I had used all the towels.

Boy, was Lola mad. After Shazam came and squeezed her off the team.

Some boys over behind the backstop hit Toby and Jimmy with the birthmark and they hit back and there was a fight in

the dust and Mrs. Winters's husband got in the middle of
them to make them stop and there was too much noise and
dust all over, I couldn't see clear who was hurt and who was
not.

Manzanita, left field

Sweet Lord Jesus save us now
Sweet Lord baby Jesus save us now
Sweet Je Je Je JeJe Je Jesus Lord
Save save save save save save save us now
Holy Jesus Lord let Thy Kingdom come on earth now
Lord come in Your glory glory Lord now
Down here on earth find us with Your glory Lord
Jesus save us now
Jesus save us now
Jesus raise us up to Your glory glory glory
Jesus save us now
Sweet sweet Jesus save us now

Hallie, right field

All that time — years — we had been curious to see
Manny get the spirit again, and some of us never even saw it
the first time. Now it was not even interesting.

What I noticed was Manny just watching everything after she was done getting the spirit. She just leaned against the backstop and watched, her face looking like she wasn't even there.

I wished I wasn't there. I kept trying to pretend it didn't happen.

Ila Mae, pitcher

Manny even got the spirit, which was no help at all. What was God gonna do now? Make the first baseman not be hurt? Make the last 5 minutes unhappen?

I watched Brita Marie and Lola and Audrey as they strove to get theirselves not kicked by Shazam. Audrey was getting the worst of it.

It was hard to pin down what my thoughts were.

Such a hullabaloo everywhere, and Manny getting the spirit over there alongside the backstop, and Hallie up against the other end of the backstop looking like she seen a ghost, it was all too awful. I picked up my glove and put it on and walked away by myself behind the bleachers which was nearly empty by now. Down behind them, there were some children playing swords and sticks. I walked around them.

I looked down at my glove and all of a sudden my conversation with Shazam about Billy Shimatsu way last autumn come into my mind. That was the little remembering I was having back there at first base but it wasn't clear then.

Now it come right to me with the cold air back on that November morning, even little Billy Shimatsu's red sweater came up in my memory. She said she might quit school because we have Japanese children. The mere sight of a Japanese made her go queasy. I suddenly found out she couldn't rise above it.

I remembered it so clear. Billy Shimatsu racing across the playground that morning, trying to keep up with Toby. I kept seeing that little first grader dashing along in his red sweater, and he kept being a terrible clue to what happened on this ball field.

I peeked through the bleachers at the commotion going on on the ball field.

I was the only one that knew.

Alva, short stop

God was the only one I knew would get the whole picture. I asked Him.

Dear God,

I know it was right for the home-plate umpire and the coaches to get together and call Brita Marie's uncle in from the outfield where he was base umpire and then all of them huddle together. It was the right thing to do, I'm not complaining.

When they had their meeting out there at the pitcher's

box, we all knew what they were doing. And we knew they would do the right thing.

But I wish we had gotten to finish our only Bat 6 game of our whole lives.

Please make that Japanese first-baseman girl not be dead. Make her not even be hurt. Make her just be fainted. Make her wake up in the ambulance way long before they get down to River Bend. Please?

I can't figure out why this bad thing happened when it was our turn in 6th grade. It never happened before. Will You explain why?

Thy will be done.

Your friend,
Alva

Ellen, shortstop

It was Piper's father, the home-plate umpire, that made the speech for all to hear. He was standing out there at the pitcher's box with the base umpire and all the coaches. He said, "It is with solemn regret we decided resulting from this tragedy on this playing field here we will not continue the game.

"We know every soul is disappointed, but that is our decision."

And it sunk in all around the ballfield. There was nary a smile in all the downheartedness. There were sounds of sadness and groaning all around, amid the dogs racing back and forth barking and rustling up the dust.

I would not get my turn at bat. Nor many others wouldn't either.

Piper's father put his hand up again and he went on talking to the crowd.

"And the Community Council is called to have a meeting in — Let's see, it's near 11 o'clock, the Council will meet by 11:10 A.M. in the Barlow School building, the principal says they can use his office, a decision will be made as quick as they can." Piper's father stopped and he looked at the other grownups around him out there at the pitcher's box. "And we ask God's guidance for the Community Council."

There was weenies forgotten on the Boy Scout fire, and there was jays getting pieces of pie from the church booths and flying off with them. And a Coke bottle that was thrown down over by third base rolled across the dust and stopped.

Then the Barlow Gospel Reverend hollered, "And will somebody get control of them dogs?"

Vernell

Mrs. Porter's face was oh so sad when we all was listening to this news, and she come right over to where I was at the visiting team bench and she said, "I'm sorry, Vernell." And she hugged me. I do not know why she hugged me. Then she begun picking up bats and gloves. I helped her. Then she stopped and sat plunk down on the bench. I sat down too. She putted her hands both up to her face and shook her head inside her hands. Then she stood up again. And she said, "Well." And then she sat down again. I stayed there beside her.

Old Louella got up out of her rocking chair with people helping her. She held her cane in her veiny hand and started walking away, with people carrying her chair and her quilt and her other things she brought to the game. I could hear her, she has a loud voice for a old lady, she said, "No standards left. No standards at all."

I said to Mrs. Porter, "How come old Louella said that?"

Mrs. Porter picked up three bats she just put down a minute before and she said, "I'm not exactly sure, Vernell. Not exactly." And she looked at me so sad. We watched old Louella leave the field.

Little Peggy

People wouldn't leave me alone. Mothers and brothers and neighbors and people I didn't know the names of, everybody was alongside me, asking me. I didn't understand any of it enough to answer them.

I kept thinking about what the Barlow coach had done when he kneeled down beside Aki, his knees down there on the baseline. He put his big old beefy hand on her arm which was spread out there, and he said, "Oh, Lordy, I'm so sorry, oh, Lordy, I'm so sorry." And he did everything Susannah's father told him to do, helping get Aki ready for the stretcher to slide under her so she could be lifted into the ambulance.

People kept asking me questions: Is Aki's jaw broken, will she be OK? Instead of answering them, I put my hands over my ears and I said, "I don't know, I don't know, I don't know." And I was crying before I even realized I was crying.

The thing that hasn't left my mind ever since is the sight of that girl not shaking Aki's hand.

Hallie

I looked over in the stands where Darlene's mom had her arm around Shazam's old grandmother who was just sitting there still as a rock.

Living out there by the gravel pit, having a problem-child granddaughter. Not even having a telephone. A pump in the kitchen. No car.

And then something in my mind popped open and I remembered. Why didn't I remember before? There was too much noise, that's why. I couldn't think in that din.

I remembered Shazam standing in my bedroom hating the Japanese and her father completely dead at the bottom of Pearl Harbor and her looking at me that way. I didn't get it then, I didn't get it till she hurt their first baseman.

I should of known. Long before. I had the whole winter and spring to figure it out.

The girl was mental.

Daisy

The noise was fierce. Some people were standing right on the third-base line arguing, and a clutter of grownups near to the pitcher's box all conversing very loud and scuffing up the dust. And one child actually threw a hot dog over at where those 3 Barlow girls were holding that one that hurt

Aki. It hit their catcher on the shoulder and splattered ketchup and mustard on her uniform.

Brita Marie

Audrey and I and Lola are different ever since that time when we held on for dear life and that girl's body was throwing itself about like a crazy person. Never again we could be children after that. I could not explain it to anybody that was not there in the grip with the 3 of us, only we know how it was. It was too creepy.

Shazam

They attacked without no warning. They are sneaky cheats they torture people even commit suicide for their country. Last time I seen my father alive I did not know it was the last time he never said no goodbye.

He went on the ship the *Arizona* they bombed his ship I never seen him again. He couldnt breathe under the bombs.

I am glad we bombed them they killed my only father.

Audrey

About the time Shazam started mumbling, she kicked my shin once too many with her heel and I let her have it. I

tightened my arms around her ribs and yelled at her from behind, "Shazam, cut it *out*! You gone ruined our game, you lay
off, you hear?" I felt it my bounden duty to say *something* to
that girl that made more trouble than anybody ever sus-
pected. I felt Coach Rayfield was busy trying to tend to the
worst parts of the trouble, it was up to somebody close by,
and I was close by. I am not ordinarily a high-strung person,
I am a patient person. Anyone would tell you I am patient.

And I helped her with arithmetic all that time. All that
whole time.

My heart was sick inside me.

And then something squishy hit me on the back and I
didn't even care what it was. Our day was ruint. Our year was
ruint.

Was our lifes ruint? I did not know. It looked like they
might be.

Brita Marie

While we were struggling to hold onto Shazam, Coach
Rayfield came over, and he tried to put his hands on her
shoulders but he could only keep a grip of part of her left
one, she was thrashing so, and he looked her in the face and
said, "Shazam, I am so ashamed."

I can tell you I would never want to show my face again
if he said that to me in such a tone of voice, I would be dis-
graced. But Shazam kept on like he wasn't even there.

And then Dotty Rayfield came and put her hand on her father's arm and said, "Let me try?"

Coach turned away looking real bitter.

Dotty Rayfield looked at Shazam in the face and she said quite calm to Audrey and Lola and me we could let go now.

We did so, but I confess I didn't really want to let go. Shazam stopped her wild thrashing and went with Dotty.

Audrey

Coach Rayfield he roamed amongst everybody. He went to the injured first baseman's father, shaking his head and saying something to him, then he done the same to the Ridge assistant coach, and then he went to the Superintendent of Schools, then he went over to two teachers who was standing by the Gospel Church booth. He looked like he said the same thing every time. He walked heavy and sorry, you had to feel for him, such a wandering apologizing man.

Wink

Some 7th graders from the Consolidated tackled our boys and they fought back, Toby and the others, for heaven's sake, Shazam wasn't *their* fault. Even Kayo Riley which doesn't fight hardly ever he had a bloody nose all over foul territory beyond third base. Some teachers was trying to get them to stop but they was not having success.

And grownups argued all over the field, very agitated in a hubbub.

Over in left field was a bunch of people being angry together. One of that crowd raised his voice up. "Girls don't do that. Girls is supposed to be ladies —"

And he got interrupted. "Could of put her eye out!"

"— could have knocked her teeth out!"

"— could of give her a brain concussion!"

"Looked to me like her eye was put out."

"Hit the ground the way she hit, a brain concussion for sure —"

"Coaches don't know how to coach anymore —"

"Gotta teach the children fair play —"

"The adults. Adults ain't fair. They set a bad example."

These chorus of grumblers went on and on and I got heavier and heavier in my stomach out there at second base. I looked around at the other girls gathered with me there and I could see nothing was making sense to them, either.

"Our coaches do too know how to coach," Ellen said, not loud.

"Ours too. He coaches very good," I said to her, also not loud.

And then none of us said anything more, we just watched over there where bunches of people was storming around. And the ambulance gone away.

Lorelei

There were many adults arguing in continuation after the Community Council went inside to have their meeting. I merely listened from second base, where none of us had left yet.

"These girls is always scalawags. But this is way beyond a scalawag. That number 7 is way far out of kilter."

"That sweet little Japanese gal, she's a credit to her race, now she's crippled for life."

"We don't know that. She might be good as new."

"Fat chance. Her head's probably bust."

One man said so loud, "That number 7 should get sent back wherever she come from. She don't belong here."

And a lady in the same gathering of people said back to him, "Give that wild child to *another* town, and her not even learned her lesson? No, we had Community Service a long, long time. Let them give her Community Service. We don't try, *no*body wins. You understand that?"

And some kept saying, "Her mother —" "She never —" "Remember her mother? That Floy?"

And some in that crowd of people were calling attention to number 7's lost soul, her not being a baptized Christian and too ignorant to know better.

And then I was so startled to hear my father, who I didn't notice was in that group till he spoke up. My father raised up his voice, loud and very clear for all around him to hear:

"This is not a case of saving souls, it's not a case of religion. In the churches there's praying to God to help kill the enemy, isn't there? And there's praying to protect the munitions factories and praying for our bombs to find their targets, isn't there? You can pray and sing, and you can preach and chant, and you can baptize till the end of time and we will still not make the world a better place till we stop all wars for all mankind.

"Every town in America would have cheered this child in 1943. In 1944. In 1945. America has told her what to be and suddenly we are completely modern in 1949 and now we revile her.

"Whose fault is this, I ask you. I say it is the fault of the United States of America and all countries that wage war through the march of history —"

My mom could not wait any longer. She squeezed into the group and she got him to quieten down. My mother is proud of what my father did being a conscientious objector for his beliefs in peace, but she makes him calm down when he gets too upset with the warfulness of his fellow mankind.

I am proud of my father's beliefs too. I am embarrassed when he yells out like that, but this time I knew his thoughts rang a bell in my heart and I understood like I had not done before.

Susannah stepped over and put her arm all the way around my shoulders. Daisy said very soft to the Barlow girls, Wink and Darlene, "That's Lorelei's father, he don't believe in war." They were all quiet and respectful to my father then. Or maybe they were quiet with embarrassment to have your own father talk out like that. I am used to that too. Or maybe they were quiet in respect of Aki being hurt so bad.

Kate

We were all standing around my base while the conniptions went on among the grownups. Amidst the shouting of one group of them, a woman said very shrill, "Just stop! Everybody stop it! Just everybody quiet down!" And they did. And she said, "We all agree it is a terrible thing she done and none of us would of done that. Everybody knows that. What are we *gonna* do is the question. What do we do now?"

Every single voice was silent.

The Community Council was having its meeting.

Tootie

I stood way off by myself and watched old Louella go home. My stomach swirled. I undid my shin guards.

It was seeing old Louella pick up and leave that made me feel so bad. Seeing that old lady that had made it through 49 games including the one she was in. Not be able to see the 50th. Made me nearly go to pieces.

But I did not go to pieces. Instead I prayed for Aki.

I looked over there at her dad and brother with Mr. Porter

and I wondered what would be right to say to them. I had just talked to God who is completely invisible and yet those 2 men and a boy were standing right on a ball field on earth and I merely held my equipment in my hands and didn't say a word.

When Susannah's mother came out of the school and told me the Community Council wanted to see me, my knees got trembly, although I am not usually a trembly person. I took off my chest protector and carried it along with my mask and knee guards.

Inside the school building it was cool and shady and quiet after the bright sun and the terrible happenings outside. I had never been in the Barlow School before, it smelled a trifle bit different, not exactly like ours, I could not exactly tell how. In the principal's office all 5 other people on the Community Council were sitting on chairs in a sort of semicircle and Susannah's mother said who I was and she sat down in the empty chair and I had to stand amongst them holding my equipment. There were the 2 preachers and Piper's mother and 2 other people I did not know.

My throat went dry.

"Tootie, you know we want to get to the bottom of this problem, don't you?" said one of the women.

I said yes and I nodded my head.

"We're wondering — Since you were in a position to know what happened in the last seconds before the incident — Did you notice anything unusual about — Oh, about the way the

Barlow player approached the batter's box, the way she held her bat, anything she might have said? Anything out of the ordinary?"

I looked around at the adults and some of them had their eyebrows raised up a little bit from the normal height.

I knew what I *might* have heard, but I didn't know what I *absolutely* heard. I didn't know if Piper's father might have heard it too. I could not say for sure if I heard anything. I sure did not hear anything clear enough to say I positively heard it.

They stared at me.

I was so mad at everything. I could just open my mouth and say what I thought I heard and that girl would be in such terrible trouble she'd never get out. I could send her to re-form school if I told what I thought I heard. She would be thrown in a stone cell and never fed. But maybe she did not say any words. Maybe she was just making sounds before hitting the ball.

And then I would grow to an old lady knowing I sent a young girl to reform school and made her be tortured.

But look what she did to Aki.

I looked at both preachers sitting on chairs waiting for me to know right from wrong. If only I heard that girl clearly, what she said. Or didn't say. If only she was completely clear in her words. If only that girl did not even make any sound when she was at bat. But she did make some sound. I knew that.

"She made a sound," I said.

"A sound with her voice, or. . . . Well, a sound with her voice?" asked the Barlow preacher.

"Yeah," I said. "Yes. A sound with her voice."

"What kind of sound, Tootie?" said the minister from our church.

It was a sound of a warning, maybe. Or maybe it was just a sound of being determined to get a hit. It was something in her voice but it was not clear enough for me to know. Something about an arbor, like that tree arbor in the minister's garden behind the church. But I could not say for sure it was that. Maybe it was not that sound, maybe it was just a sound of a batter getting ready to swing.

"I don't know."

"Are you sure you don't know?" another man asked.

I looked inside my heart. I still could not be sure I heard any sound I understood. I could pretend I was sure and send her to reform school.

I said yes, I was sure. "It was a sound. I don't know what kind of sound."

They looked around at one another. Then Susannah's mother said, "Is there anything else you can tell us, Tootie? Anything else you saw or heard?"

No. There wasn't. Not anything.

The Community Council called in many people after me. It took hours.

Brita Marie

Never in my life did I think I would stand in front of the Community Council.

All the time I was in there I kept seeing Shazam on the first day of school, in that tablecloth dress and those ugly brown shoes from the rummage sale.

They asked me, "How well do you know Shirley, Brita Marie?"

I told them she makes sure everybody calls her Shazam. Some of the grownups didn't know the word and I had to explain about Captain Marvel. "It's the magic word, it's Captain Marvel power." I told them about when she came to Barlow. "The first day she ever came to our school, she was alone there by the flagpole. . . . I felt sorry for her. We all felt — It was a combination of sorry and mystery." I thought but did not say how pitiful she looked with that dress and those shoes.

"We found out she could hit left- and right-handed, and throw both too. We thought God sent her to us. I don't know who said it first. We all thought it, I guess."

They sat there looking at me and thinking.

The Gospel Reverend asked, "What if someone did not want to call Shirley this name Shazam?"

I said how it was better to call her that. "But Mrs. Winters, she always calls her Shirley," I said.

They kept asking if I could think what got into her head to do such a thing. I kept saying I didn't even have any idea. After a while, they let me go.

Audrey

All together totaled up the number of people that had to answer questions to the Community Council was nearly a dozen. Including Shazam's old grandmother and Shazam herself.

They didn't get no more out of her than a stone.

While Brita Marie was in there I sat on the bleachers and waited to walk home with her. The ambulance had probably got to the hospital by then.

Many people had went home in disappointment after the umpire's announcement. My parents and my grandmother had gone home. The ball field was nearly empty, just some folks at the booths. And some Boy Scouts looking after their fire.

We would go down in history as the team with such bad behavior we had to have our game stopped. We would have trouble to hold our heads up over such disgrace. I kept saying to myself, We won't finish our game, it is all over.

Over at the Gospel Church table where there was still foods for sale but nobody was buying them, several grownups was talking so I could hear, including my great-uncle Beau. I will repeat what they said, I remember it that clear:

"She's one of God's forgotten children, that number 7."

"No she ain't. The Lord didn't forget that one. The Lord loves her just as much as anybody. Maybe more."

"Yeah! More! She's a lost lamb, He —"

And Uncle Beau interrupted with his big voice: "You none of you are paying any attention! This ain't a case of the Lord, it ain't a case of no lost lambs — this is a case of somebody *hurt* somebody."

In my private mind I agreed with Uncle Beau, not just because he is my uncle. But I also was thinking about how Shazam should of had some of the Lord's love before things got out of hand.

One of the other people over there shook her head and said, "Jesus died for that child's sins. . . ."

Now, I do not know if this was supposed to help solve the problem of that girl loaded in the ambulance, or it meant Shazam would get forgave by God.

A thing that made me so sad I would not of been able to speak if anybody wanted me to was this: There would be no "Beautiful for Spacious Skies" this year to end the game. In 1948 we all sung it with the Gospel Church choir director leading with her arms.

I hummed a short piece of it all by myself, there on the bleachers. It was the "God shed His grace on thee" part.

It made me feel a little bit better, it is a pretty song of our land.

My great-uncle Beau, what would he paint on the big board over at the Flying Horse gas station?

Shazam

Dotty Rayfield come to my rescue when those girls was manhandling me she said to me I could come with her now. You can come with me now Shazam she said. They let go my arms Audrey let go my chest where she was holding me too tight. Dotty Rayfield she says lets walk over there she points her head to the stump way back almost to the blackberry tangle. So we walked out there Dotty Rayfield she was holding my arm. Not any grabbing like those girls done that I thought was my friends of the Pioneer Team.

Dotty Rayfield said how come did I hit that girls head. I did not know how come so I did not say. Dotty Rayfield kept saying to me there is a hurt girl in a ambulance going to a hospital did I understand and how come did I make her get hurt. I did not say nothing to Dotty Rayfield she brang me back where I had to go to the principals office.

I was running I could not breathe my elbow come up.

In the principals office they was 6 grownups said how come did I hurt that girl.

The Japs killed my only father I ever had. They was mean

faces sitting on them chairs I did not say that word to them I shut up my face.

They asked me was I happy at Barlow I did not say.

They said theres a girl in a hospital did I understand. I said yes.

They kept asking me did I this was I that. I did not say.

I couldnt breathe too many Jap faces there was one over there at first base my elbow come up.

Ila Mae

It was my fault. I should of told. I should of told some-body. Mrs. Winters. Coach Rayfield. Audrey. Darlene. Beautiful Hair. My mother. The Gospel Reverend. Somebody.

I selfishly kept it hid all that whole time from November to May 28th and would not of told anybody even then. Not even then. Not if I did not have to by God telling me to do so. God told me I had to let this bad secret out. It took me a long time to do it, many days after May 28. But I done it. I did it.

Lola and Lila

We knew. We *knew.* We knew there was something wrong with her. We should have told somebody. We should have said right at Wink's party, "You peeked, you should not get the prize." We were afraid to stand up for the right thing, instead we went along with everybody else and we was nice to her when we should not have been nice.

She came in here to our town and took over. Everybody got different. Audrey was her math teacher and then Wink too. Hallie had her over. Darlene was always so generous to her. We all was. Every single one of us made extra room in our daily life for her.

We knew it and we should have told.

We did not even tell our parents which if we did they would do something to make justice. Then this never would happen, this bad horrible thing to send a person to the hospital, maybe dead.

Hallie

We went home in poor spirits like I don't remember we ever got since my dad's bad injury. My dad and my mom were in the pickup and me and my sister sat in the back, leaning up against the cab.

My sister kept saying, "This never happened before. It shames us all."

She said it and she said it, and I got mad and I told her, "We already know that. Don't you think we already know that? We already feel bad enough. You don't have to rub it in so bad." I took off the good-luck socks and I put them back in my sister's hand and left my shoes beside the cab. Then I slid across all the wood chips to the very back end of the pickup and hung my head over to look at the road going away underneath. It was just a road like normal everyday life. You'd never know such a terrible thing happened if you just kept your eyes down there staring at the road going by.

Before I even had a chance to change out of my Pioneer uniform, my dad wanted me to go out walking with him in the field between the woodshed and the woods. Being out there gave me the willies, remembering him hitting fungoes to me and Shazam in the sunshiny, cold afternoon way last fall.

I walked on my dad's good-hearing side like usual, and he started right away to tell me his important thing.

"That day I took Shirley home after we practiced out here, you remember?" he said to me. I said Sure I remember. "She said something in the pickup, I was never sure I heard her right. I'll tell you what she said." He stopped walking, so I did too. I looked up at him out from under the shade of my Pioneer cap. He said, "She must've seen Mr. Utsumi. Or Mrs. Were they there?"

I thought back to that cold, shivery afternoon. Shazam had climbed in the pickup after my dad got it started, and they drove away.

What else? Oh yeah: My mom came out on the porch to say good-bye. Were the Utsumis there? I couldn't remember.

"I don't know. What did she say?" I said up to him.

My dad looked way off to the place where the grouse

have their nest in the spring. "They must've been there. Or one of them."

And I remembered the ginger smell. "Yes! Mom brought out cookies, the ginger kind — she had two sacks, one for the Utsumis and one for Shazam, and she gave one to Shazam and she handed me the other to give to old Mr. Utsumi by the fence. Why was he there?"

"I don't remember. Was he really there, Hallie? Tell me for sure." My dad was urgent.

"Yes. He was for sure there. I gave him the sack of cookies and he said thanks and he went off home." He carried the sack of cookies, leaning on his tall walking stick with his bent posture from being so old and from having his son die. When he got partway across the field, he stopped and ate a cookie out of the bag and then he turned around to wave to my mom, but she'd gone back inside off the cold porch, and he stood there waving to the empty yard.

"What did Shazam say?" I asked him again. "In the pickup."

"Oh, I ain't sure she even said it. What I *thought* she said —" He stopped and kept looking at the grouse nest territory in the woods.

"Well, what did you *think* she said?"

"Hallie, I just never was sure. I couldn't hear clear with the engine running. . . ." He turned directly toward me and lowered his voice. "I thought I heard her say, 'You could get that Jap.'"

In my shock I just looked at my dad.

"But I couldn't hear her clear. I never knew if she really said that or not." My dad looked down at me serious. "I've carried a heavy heart, Hallie. It's never left me, what she said. Only I never knew if she did say it — or if she didn't."

I put my arms around my dad there in the field. He felt so bad. "What did you say back to her?" I asked his hearing side.

"I told her they're our neighbors. I said, 'Shirley, they're our *neighbors*.' But then I wondered if I'd heard her wrong, and I just drove her on home." My dad stood so still with me hugging him. "Maybe if I'd said something then. If I'd told Coach Rayfield. Or the principal. Or anybody. I've carried a heavy heart."

I kept my arms around my dad. There was nothing we could do now.

But in the middle of the night I woke up and remembered Mr. Utsumi, exactly why he was there that afternoon. I went to my mom and dad's room, I could see just the shapes of them asleep. I shook my dad awake very gentle. He turned his head so he had his good ear up and I told him there in the dark. "Mr. Utsumi was bringing back the hay fork, remember? He had it all mended, a new handle put in the shaft, he was bringing back the hay fork. That day."

And my dad he breathed out hard and he whispered to me, "Oh, yeah, I remember. The hay fork. Yeah. I remember." And he shook his head for sadness there in the dark.

13	BEAR CREEK RIDGE GRADE SCHOOL
AND	**BARLOW ROAD GRADE SCHOOL**

Little Peggy

When they said Aki didn't die I had known it already in my heart; I personally was not surprised. I knew God wouldn't take away my best friend; I knew that wouldn't be a reasonable thing for God to do.

Her horrible injuries, her head and neck in the huge brace, her having to not move and not talk for so many weeks that the summer would be over by the time she could be regular again — her not remembering what had happened at the game — all that was terrible like a nightmare. But it wasn't as terrible as what might have happened.

I had never prayed so hard for anything.

Shadean

Only a few good things happened from that worst day of our lives:

Our two teams got to know each other by emergency. We were all in that terrible mess together, and the score will remain tied till our dying day, and we got acquainted in our resentfulness. Mr. and Mrs. Porter said us girls were very brave and grown-up in the question of we did not let our unfinished Bat 6 ruin our lives.

It is hot summer now and several girls even went trout fishing together that did not know each other till May 28.

And Aki's father's deer fence is getting built slow but sure by the work of that girl Shirley with the bad psychology.

Many adults say we have learned a bad lesson of race prejudice and we will always remember it. Well, I would rather not learn this lesson because of what Aki has to go through.

Especially, I got to know Hallie on the Barlow team who is so nice and we got jobs together for the summer, hoeing berries in Hirokos' berry patch. And then picking when they got ripe. And I promise I'll never call her Beautiful Hair. But her hair is knockout beautiful all down her back.

Hallie needs a friend, on account of she knew a little bit of that lunatic girl's crazy mind. She just didn't know enough. Hallie feels burdened with her guilt but we get in good spirits together. So much that Mr. Hiroko comes and tells us to keep our minds on our work.

Hallie went with me to Aki's one day, we took her a Wonder Woman comic book and a whole bunch of forget-me-nots, even though she had so many flowers all over her room already.

Wink

My list, I had everything on a list, it ain't any good anymore. Things didn't go like my list.

These 2 towns never been so upset before. In the Barlow Store Audrey's grandmother said, standing right beside the oleomargarine, "We fought that war so all races could live fair! Hitler was the one that did that to people that had different faces. Not us. We don't do that in America!"

And right away, Manzanita's father said, "In America they do it to them Negroes all the time. That gal she just did it out in the open for all to see."

And then Miss James, the third-grade teacher Alva worked so hard for to earn money for her softball glove, she was in the store too, buying a new mop for her floor, and she up and said, "We put the Japanese in those camps. We do too do it in America. Forgive me for saying so, but I am ashamed."

Manny's father might be a little bit odd on account of his daughter gets the spirit, so people don't listen to him much. But all the same, he is right about the Negroes. Even Jackie Robinson has people yelling at him to get off the white man's field. So I agreed with Miss James, although I did not say so out loud.

And besides, Manny's father mended the backstop almost by himself in time for our game that never got finished, so he can't be completely wrong.

I am still mad my list didn't work out. I don't think Hank Greenberg ever had anything this terrible happen to him.

But there is a good part. I am mixed about admitting it happened while that poor girl lain in the hospital. But it did. Daisy which played third base for the Ridge, and Lorelei which was their center field, invited me to be their friend. They are the nicest girls and Lorelei has real paintings in her house.

But then just as sudden as I got these new friends there was the problem about Daisy and the Catholic school.

Kate

Well, my dad he got so riled up he took matters unto his own hands and said us girls should not go to school with a criminal girl and he said he would not send me to the Consolidated. He would school me at home better than have me contaminated. Contaminate my mind, that's what he said. He would let the boys go to school because they do not have riffraff in their grades, but me he would keep home.

But my mom rolled her eyes. She did not have hardly any schooling on account of being poor. Now for me to have not hardly any on account of one bad apple, she said it was plain foolishness and my dad would just need some time to get unexcited over it.

My dad called around other parents and tried to get them to say it was either her or us. He wanted everybody to agree on if she stayed we none of us would go to the Consolidated. He got on the phone with the Superintendent of Schools who said he could not forbidden a child to attend the Consolidated unless they got sent to reform school which that girl did not. My dad was so mad he hung up on him.

Only Daisy's and Ellen's and Alva from down in Barlow's parents agreed with my dad, and for 11 whole days they were arranging how to school us.

Daisy would go to the Catholic School down past River Bend, me and Ellen and Alva could go too, even with it being a different religion. We would get to wear uniforms and they have mean nuns and nice nuns. Daisy said 7th grade has a nice one, and I got all mixed feelings about it. Uniforms would be pretty, but we would not see our friends, and our lifes would change.

Then all our parents found out it would cost $245.00 for just one year of schooling down there. My dad said it was a outrage and corruption, and the final result of it was we will all get to go to the Consolidated after all.

Well, my dad was not happy about it, he predicted that child would be nothing but trouble from here to kingdom come.

It was the day after all that confusion ended, my mom said I was such a grouch I should just get on my bike and blow off steam and not come home till I could be nice at supper. So I did. I just kept riding and being mad, and this is what happened:

I was riding down the road that goes past the Barlow Gospel Church, where the little bridge crosses the East Fork, and I just rode along and I rode along and about a half mile after the bridge I saw a bike laying on the crick bank where it curves to the west. Down the bank from where the bike was, the Barlow team pitcher, Ila Mae, was sitting beside the crick and she was sobbing and crying and carrying on, and I put my bike beside the other one and I went down the bank to where she was sitting there all alone crying, and this is what I found out.

Ila Mae was on her way riding home from the Gospel Reverend, she had gone to see him for help and comfort. She was mad at him, she was mad at that number 7 Shazam, she was mad at herself most of all, and she was crying all down her T-shirt.

What she told me was a true surprise and I would feel bad too if I was her. Ila Mae and Shazam had a conversation way last November when Shazam saw a Japanese first grader and she said that bad word that begins with a J. Ila Mae should of told somebody right away and then the tragedy of our Bat 6 game would not of happened because maybe Shazam would not be allowed to play in the game.

Instead of telling somebody Shazam had race prejudice, Ila Mae told her not to say that bad word. "I told her she wouldn't get to play in our game if she said that word. And I *thought* I was telling her we don't have no race prejudice here. I thought I was doing that also." Ila Mae was so crying mad, and she was digging in the mud with a stick, and she said, "I *thought* I was doing the right thing, and now it turns out I was doing the wrong thing, and I didn't even know it, and I ruined the game for everybody, and I have to wait till I die to find out if God forgave me, and —"

And I put my arm around her back and I said, "You didn't know. You didn't know what was the right thing to do, you did your best."

Ila Mae continued her mad crying and said, "And the Gospel Reverend says God forgives every single sinner there is, but he don't know if God will forgive me right away. We don't really know God's forgiveness till we're dead and *then* we find out did we get sent up to Heaven or down there to Satan. Then I asked him does God forgive Shazam too, and the Gospel Reverend said Not till she is a babitized Christian, and I'm so mad at her I don't even *care* if she gets forgave by God, and that makes me a worse sinner than I already was." And Ila Mae who pitched so good in that one inning we got to play was dripping in tears.

"I didn't tell the Community Council about that conversation way last fall, and it was bad of me not to. I kept it in my heart till I couldn't keep it in no longer, and now I took my secret of it to the Gospel Reverend for help, he says he is always there for our help. So I told him about it in my hope to be forgave, and he tells me I won't know till I'm dead!"

I did not know anything to do. I stared into the water going over the little rocks and waving the grasses and I felt bad for all of us. We will all be in the 7th grade together over at the Consolidated High School in the autumn, and now was as good a time as any to be a new friend to poor Ila Mae. In fact, it was the best time.

"I forgive you," I said to Ila Mae.

"What's your name?" she said with her dripping face looking at me.

"Kate," I said.

"Kate," she said. She looked back down at the water. "I ran your base."

"Yeah," I said. "I know who you are," I told her. "You're Ila Mae, you pitched real good."

And that compliment made her cry all over again. "We all feel bad," I reminded her. "And like our coaches said, it will not ruin our lifes. We got our whole lifes to live." I took my arm off her shoulder and threw a couple of little pebbles in the crick.

Ila Mae wrote my name Kate in the mud with her stick. She said my hair is real pretty red and I said thanks. I think we are going to be friends. I would really love to have her come over to my house. We could make Popsicles in our freezer compartment and we could also put on my mom's lipstick and leave kiss marks on the mirror.

But when I think how I was so happy about the refrigerator at Christmas and now everything is so bad, I know it was really dumb to think a refrigerator could be so important. We have our new refrigerator and our Bat was ruined.

Ila Mae and me are going to be excellent friends.

Hallie

I never saw a man feel so bad as my dad feels about not telling anybody what Shazam said in the pickup way last fall. He feels it is his fault "nobody knew in time." Even when he went on his own free will to the Community Council and told in front of them all, and they said this was understandable, not to tattletale on a child if you weren't even sure you heard what the child said anyway.

He says, "I had the clue. And I kept it to myself. I did not do justice and I feel ashamed."

My mom and even my sister say not to be so hard on himself, but my dad walks around forlorn.

Me, I feel bad too. Terribly bad. But I get comforted knowing Shadean and me get to work together for the Hirokos. I wonder if the Hirokos hate me for being on the same team with crazy Shazam. Mr. Hiroko might hate me and never even let on. You would never know just talking to him.

Shazam

It is easy for them all to be niceynice. They got everything they need they dont know how its like without no father and not have a real home.

I dig the post holes straight no crooked ones it is hot out there. A Jap face tells me where to dig and stretches the wire tight with me. He is a boy boss I dont look in his face. Nobody has to work hard as much as me I get so hungry I could eat more than that little bitty lunch Grammama sends me along. He said did I want some of his lunch I said him no answer. Them Japs killed my father.

His Jap name is Shig and he says These holes are good and straight Shazam. You did them real carefully good for you. I dont say nothing. Its hard to breathe but I do my work good.

They made me do 200 hours of Community Service all hours of Jap families. First is the ones that first baseman gone to the hospital. I have to work till their whole deer fence is made all around their orchard on two sides by the woods where the deer live. I never seen no deer.

The Community Council said to me did I understand and I said yes. I said yes so they let me go.

They told my Grammama my Community Service hours she said how she is ashamed. I didnt say nothing to her neither. She gets her headaches.

Aki

When they told me on June 2nd that I had been lifted on a stretcher into the River Bend ambulance and that was how I got to the hospital and my mother had been with me the whole ride down the highway, I was surprised. I didn't remember any of that. And then they told me on June 3rd there was a hubbub on the playing field on May 28th. Everyone said there was no need to be embarrassed, it's not my fault, but still I was embarrassed.

I can't move my head because of all the braces around it.

Everyone said I had a strange way of thinking about the accident. For one thing, I was glad Little Peggy had to be the Bear Creek Ridge speller in the county spelling bee. She won the county bee. Then when she went to the Oregon State Spelling Bee in the capital, she came in fifth. The word she missed was "commensurate."

And also that number 7 who hit me. They have asked me if I want to hit her back and I say no. I mean I write "No." I'm not allowed to talk until the end of the summer. And I can't shake my head in the brace.

It was a bad thing for her to do, but like they say, forgive your enemies. It is true she didn't have a good spirit about playing the game. But when they told me how mixed up that girl was I felt sorry for her. It would be terrible to have your father dead from a bomb. That whole war was very bad.

And then there is my wired jaw. I can't eat solid food. But it has advantages too. Many of the girls are out working hard picking strawberries in the hot sun, but I am sitting at home in bed with mashed strawberries put through a sieve and fed to me like liquid.

Still, it hurts quite a lot. I get headaches and I have to suck a dissolved aspirin through a straw.

My bedroom is full of dogwood both white and pink, and red, yellow, and white tulips, poppies of two colors, and purple anemones. Every time people bring me flowers my mother has to find more canning jars to put them in.

One of the worst things is the girls who come to visit having to see our bad house. This is the most embarrassing. The walls are stained from the renters that weren't careful. I don't know why anyone would throw soup at a wall, but when we came back we had to scrape noodles off the wallpaper in the living room. And our cupboards without doors on them because they got pulled off. The girls pretend they don't notice how bad it looks around here. They keep their eyes on the flowers they are bringing and they also keep looking down at the paper where I write the notes to answer what they ask me.

My grandmother bows to everyone who comes to visit. She has bowed to people all her life, it is her habit. When the minister from the church comes, when Mr. and Mrs. Porter come, she bows to them. They're getting used to bowing back.

Mrs. Winters, the sixth-grade teacher at Barlow, came to see me, bringing a bouquet of gentians from her garden. She said that in her five years of teaching she had never seen such a thing as what happened in Bat 6. She said she felt terrible.

She asked what she could do to make it up to me. I didn't know. She said she felt it was somehow her fault for not knowing. I wrote her a note that said I didn't see how it could be her fault. She cried. She and my grandmother bowed to each other coming and going.

My grandmother bowed to the Barlow coach, Mr. Rayfield, and he stood in the doorway looking so uncomfortable and he bowed back to her. He looked as if he had never bowed before. He sat on the chair in my bedroom and told me how bad he felt, but mainly he told me I was a good ball player. He said, "Honest, if I'da *known*." I already had a note saying "It's OK" sitting right beside my bed, because I have to say it so often. But I wrote him a new one. It would have been rude to give him a wrinkled note that had been used so many times before.

"No, it's not okay," he said to me. He looked so nervous. "Our center field, she went over the brink. I mean, look at you here. Look at you."

I couldn't look at me, my head was immobilized in the brace.

He gave my mother three jars of peach jam that his wife has made. He said to my mom, "Boy, I wish I'd seen you play back then. Back when you were MVP. I sure wish I'd been there."

My mom said, "Thank you."

He left still feeling bad.

My mom is so mad. But she won't let anyone see how mad she is. She won't even let me find out. But I know anyway. How could I not know? Even her feet are mad, I can hear them being mad on the floor.

Lorelei brought me a new Nancy Drew book and a snapshot her father had taken with his camera before I got hurt. There we were, the Mountaineers together as a team on the visitors' bench, all ready to play our Bat 6. Lorelei said to me, "I halfway didn't want to bring this picture and make you feel bad. But I brought it anyway to make you feel good."

It hurt so bad when I laughed, Lorelei felt terrible. I am not supposed to laugh until August, the doctor says. That was the operating doctor down at the hospital in River Bend who said that, not Susannah's father.

Susannah's father came to the hospital each day at first, bringing my mother or father with him every time. Then when I came home he came every alternate day for a while.

The get-well cards are extremely embarrassing. There are too much of them, in piles everywhere. The huge cardboard one from the whole sixth grade has everybody's name on it, even all the boys. It is propped against the wall.

And there is a special card from the whole Barlow Pioneers team with every girl's name on it. That center-field girl's name isn't on the card.

So many people volunteered to drive that girl up to our

orchard five days each week and drive her home again after her eight hours of work on the deer fence are finished. Mrs. McHenry is one of the main volunteers, being so involved as she was with the team and the sixth grade and our orchard and our house. She felt the worst of anybody about what those drunk renters had done to our house.

Shig told me Shirley is a hard worker and the post holes she dug with the post-hole digger were just right after she got the hang of it. And she is good at mixing the concrete, too. Of course Shig is mad, too, but he just goes ahead and works on the fence.

Another embarrassing thing is how many prayers they say up at the church. Every single Sunday the minister prays for me to get well, just the same as he is praying for peace in Korea. Everyone who goes to church gives me the report on the prayers. I kind of wish they would stop.

Still, I wake up in the night and I wonder why it had to be me.

Little Peggy

I personally wanted Aki to come right out and say — I mean write in a note — she was so mad at that crazy girl for hurting her and sending her to the hospital. I thought it was abnormal she was not really mad.

I sat there beside her bed and I told her that and I've never gotten mad at Aki before in my life but I thought I was going to. I felt myself getting hot in my face, reading her note that said, "It's not so bad. I'll get well and I still have my friends and we'll have a good time in 7th grade."

I started to say, "Aki, you're crazy not to be mad at her —"

And Aki wrote me another note then, and it had words I didn't know, they are Japanese words, and then English words:

"*Shikata ga nai.* There is nothing to be done about it."

And I said in excitement, "Aki, I *know* that. That's not the point. Can't you at least get mad?"

And then she wrote me a note that mystified me: "That is the point."

And because I was mystified I just asked her how to say those words. And she showed me on the paper how to say them. I practiced them there in her bedroom and then I said good-bye and I got on my bike and went home.

I never heard Aki say any Japanese words before that time. Or since, either.

It's so frustrating not to be able to understand how my best friend thinks.

What makes me so mad to this day is how I didn't say anything when that girl refused to shake Aki's hand before the game. If I'd said anything right then. Even with Aki like usual not getting upset. If I'd said to Mrs. Porter — or to any-body — "that girl refused to shake Aki's hand."

I'll remember that for the rest of my life.

Brita Marie

Shazam's old grandmother is the one I feel sorry for. With her sadness about what her own granddaughter did. She's all alone out there by the gravel pit, and Lord knows how she gets through each day.

Shazam did not have any upbringing till she came over here to her grandmother's. And she went and ruined things.

That mother, Floy, came over here to visit again but she didn't take Shazam away with her. Shazam has her Community Service to do, she could not leave town till that is done. And it looks like her mom is not adequate for upbringing anyway.

It's better if Floy isn't around here. How could a person that sunk so low ever show her face in town? Her old mother would be worse off than before, with another mouth to feed.

Wink

Crazy Shazam is paying the price for her meanness, but the price ain't high enough if you want my opinion.

It is too bad her mother and dad never got married, it is not her fault she is a illegitimate. But that don't mean she can hold a grudge on the whole Japanese race and bang the brains out of a girl on a ball field.

Nobody speaks to her, she is a outcast. Nobody goes out by the gravel pit to see her, and Coach Rayfield made her turn in her red Pioneer cap which there's a rule we get to keep for our whole lifetimes. Just think of that: All over Barlow and Bear Creek Ridge and even elsewhere there is old faded caps in people's memory books, and Shazam ain't got hers.

Good. I'm glad.

Lola and Lila

The Community Council proposed a new rule for the Bat and all grownups had to go to either the Barlow Store or up to McHenrys' and vote on it. From now until eternity, any act of bad sportsmanship in the Bat 6 game will make the game terminate on the spot with no winner.

Those men on the Barlow Store porch with that crippled-leg dog watched everybody going in and out of the store for the vote, and they grumbled about kids today, "barbaric" was what they said. They acted like it was trespassing on the store porch when their radio was on the ballgames where they were listening to that Negro Brooklyn Dodger Jackie Robinson stealing bases.

We are very mad about not getting to play in our game, and it is a good thing we have long lives to live with many happy things to look forward to.

Poor Piper's father still feels bad about that game and he is thinking about never umpiring again. He regrets he didn't see it coming, that terrible thing Shazam did.

We were not treated fair, especially Lola.

We were nice to her the whole year long and look what she did.

And Brita Marie. She was the first one to lay eyes on Shazam. Brita Marie gets all A's and she didn't notice anything. How come she didn't?

Susannah

I knew Darlene would be a good friend. Every time her mother comes to clean for us Darlene comes too and we are making a garden beside the pond with a rock wall holding it up, and my parents are paying us to do it. It gets hot and we go wading in the pond and we have picked many cattails.

Darlene and I took Aki a huge bunch of cattails standing in a milk can. She has hundreds of flowers in her room.

Darlene still doesn't have her own bedroom. She uses sloppy grammar which my parents will not ever let me use. Not even once. I said, "It's okay for Darlene to say it but not me? How come?"

And my mom and dad both sat me down for a lecture. Getting sat down by both of them at once is not fun, even though they always tell me how fair they are being. The grammar lecture: It is okay for Darlene to say "has went," and "never no more" and "ain't." That is because Darlene hasn't had the opportunities my little brother and I have.

Darlene doesn't have opportunities because her family is not lucky to have as much education. Darlene is just as good a person as I am but she and I will do different things in life. Like what? I ask. They say they don't know. What will Darlene do? They say they don't know.

To me they don't make sense.

Darlene and I have the same favorite colors and flowers. We made a giant chain of both purple and white clover and we took it to Aki. She writes notes instead of talking. She wrote, "This huge clover chain is beautiful and I love it, thank you." She could wear it like a Hawaiian lei if she did not have so much equipment around her head.

I wonder in secret: Would Darlene and me be good friends like we are if our game had gotten to be completely played and somebody had won? We will never know.

That could drive me batty. Wondering.

It's so terrible about Aki. But down inside I still am glad it wasn't me.

Audrey

You never saw a man go through what poor Coach Rayfield has went through. He is a man toiled with sorrow. People are saying he should of seen it coming with Shazam being so different the whole time. He feels like a guilty man that sold the soul of his girls by not predicting what Shazam would do when she got in the game and her mind went.

The third-grade teacher told Alva and Alva told Brita Marie and me that Coach Rayfield wants somebody else to coach the Bat for the year of 1950. He is sick at heart and Mrs. Rayfield will not even go in the Barlow Store for her groceries. She sent in her voting ballot for the new Bat 6 rule of bad sportsmanship, she would not go where people are. She has not gone to church also for 7 Sundays.

Dotty Rayfield has composed herself very good, though. She is working in the packing house like always, boxing cherries for shipping. Her station in the packing-line rotation is right behind my mom and Dotty Rayfield has her old regular spirits back like usual, my mom said. "It's not anybody's fault when a child goes off like that," she said to my mom. "Everybody has tried real hard to be good to her, everybody's gone out of their way for her. Out of their way. She needs remorse which she has not got. My dad will have to learn it's not his fault. He's a stubborn man, my dad. Both Mom and me wish he would see the reality of it, but he won't. Not yet. He needs time."

It is sad when a man can't make peace in his heart.

Lorelei

What happened with my dad on the day of the Bat that never got to be played to the end was amazing but Daisy said she was not amazed. It started when our car battery was dead and we couldn't go home.

And guess who came over to give the battery a jump start, it was Daisy's father, he walked over just as normal as could be, he backed their pickup over by our car, and he hooked up some cables and wires and our car started.

And Daisy's father said to my dad, "Now you be sure you keep it running. You can't let it die or you'll have the same trouble again. . . ."

And my dad said to him, "Thank you. I know we haven't agreed. . . ."

And Daisy's father said, "Well, it ain't serious enough to set a bad example for the kids. . . ." And he stuck out his hand for my dad to shake.

They shook hands there beside the ball field on that unluckiest day of our girlhood. I saw them do it, and I didn't say anything. But later Daisy and I got on the phone and said "Hooray" together for the peace our fathers made.

We think their good feelings are not just for this short time, we think they will be friendly forever. When the whole town took up the collection to help the Mikamis pay their giant hospital bills, my dad and Daisy's dad went out together in Daisy's dad's car, which works much better than ours. They went to many neighbors up and down 4 roads, and nearly everybody said yes they would give some money.

Aki's father was so surprised when he got the great big check from the whole town. And down in Barlow they were collecting too. Mr. Mikami tried to refuse the money, but he was not let to do it by the towns trying to help in time of need. The whole accident cost way more than $100.00. It's shocking.

Ellen

That's why they kept harping on the war all the time. Why didn't they *say* so? Why didn't they tell us *why* we had to remember about the war? We would of *known*. Why didn't Mrs. Porter or somebody just say to us, "Look, girls, there are abnormal people that have damaged brains and they make revenge on the war." We would of under*stood*.

I asked my mom why nobody explained it to us before.

My own mom that worked in the shipyards didn't know the answer.

My own dad said, "I thought you *did* know."

"Well, I didn't. So there," I said.

And he said, "Don't you dare be rude in this house, young lady."

Well, he was so stunned himself that the pictures he took at the game did not turn out because he dropped the camera when the hullaballoo began.

Mr. and Mrs. Porter had a meeting of all of us with all our parents and they said we mustn't let this tragic happening ruin our girlhood, we are supposed to be mature and not be sulking children. What was done was done, and we should all get ready to be 7th graders over at the Consolidated in the fall. Of course Aki could not go to the meeting, she can't move.

Well, it was not that easy. We were mad.

"Getting mad doesn't do any good," they said.

Some of the parents were so mad, they wouldn't stop arguing. It was awful.

But Daisy's father and Lorelei's father sat beside each other at the meeting. That was so good, to see those men forgive and forget. They made an example of themselves for all to see.

But still. We had our indoor bathroom and our fridge but Aki had her head in a brace and she couldn't say a single word. Sometimes couldn't you just hate the world?

14	**BEAR CREEK RIDGE GRADE SCHOOL**
AND	**BARLOW ROAD GRADE SCHOOL**

Brita Marie

Manzanita's lost her marbles. She rode on her bike on a Sunday afternoon, out by the gravel pit, and she parked her bike beside the path and she knocked on Shazam's old grandmother's door and said she'd come to visit.

Out of the blue.

She actually went to visit that girl that ruined everything for us.

I don't get it. Nobody gets it.

Manzanita

God told me to. On the morning of July 17, in the bathtub before Sunday School, Jesus walked on the water, like a miniature Jesus, and he come right up to me and he said I should befriend Shazam.

I knew I would make the others mad by doing such a thing.

But I could not not do what Jesus told me to.

So I rode my bike out there to see Shazam. Even a criminal has a right to have a friend.

I wished I would not of gone to see her. She still didn't get it.

She showed me a necklace of little white shells from Hawaii that her father give her when she was little tiny. I said they were real pretty. To tell the truth, they weren't much. It only looked like a dime-store necklace. I did not say it to her face. To her those dinky little shells were such a big deal. I think if your father loved you he would give you a nicer gift.

She said we could go out to the gravel pit and throw rocks at birds. I said I didn't want to. I thought how Wink said Shazam never did have married parents, I imagine her brain don't work right on account of that.

I come home feeling worse than before.

But then Jesus come to me again while I was pouring out milk for the kittens on the porch. He said, "Manzanita child of God, Christian goodness ain't easy, you try again." Oh, brother. I set down on the porch and I hung my head. And right there on the porch step Jesus said, "Be of good courage, Manny." And he went away like always.

This time I did it different. On a Saturday morning I woke up and God said to me, "Manny, you have the gumption of the Lord, now use it."

So I borrowed Brita Marie's bike. I told her I couldn't explain then, I would explain later, and she said OK. I walked both my bike and hers all the way out there to Shazam's old grandmother's house.

I told Shazam we was going bike riding and her grandmother said OK. She mostly just works in her garden and she does not say much. She is too ashamed I guess.

Well, we went along the road, Shazam is so strong she did not get tired going up the hill from the Flying Horse station, she said how good Brita Marie's bike was. I did not know when she would start to figure out where we was going. Well, it was when we went across the crick for the second time. She started to turn Brita Marie's bike around, and I said to her, "Look, Shazam, this is for your own good. Don't you know you don't go see that girl you can't even *live* here anymore?" I made that up on the spot.

Shazam looks at me. I know she don't have any place else to go.

"You know you don't go along with me you ain't going to get to go to the Consolidated with us? You could end up in reform school." We were coming over the little rise of the road that goes to that first baseman's house, right alongside their orchard trees. Before Shazam did that terrible thing I did not know who Aki Mikami was or where she lived, but everybody knows now.

"How come you think you got power over me?" says Shazam in her way.

Then I did a thing God will just have to forgive me for. I said, "Jesus give me the power, it's magic, you have to go see that girl or you're in bigger trouble than before, you'll get 900 hours and reform school too. So there, Shazam, think about that." I knew God was listening to me telling those lies, and I also knew this girl was so ignorant of the Lord's way she didn't know the difference. I hope God has forgave me by now.

We got to the Mikamis' orchard driveway where their mailbox is held up by the prettiest polished wood stand I ever seen, it has a pot of bright red geraniums in like a bracket right beside the mailbox.

I trusted God to help me. I did not know what would happen now.

We parked the bikes beside the house and I said to her in a undervoice, "You stick with me, don't you dare budge, you hear?" And she did so.

Being as it was warm weather their door was open, with just a rattly screen door to knock on and I did. A old lady opened it up and bowed to us both and I bowed back but Shazam she just stared in her way of no good manners training. Me and Shazam stepped on in.

Imagine anybody bowing to that girl. It could make my blood boil. But I was on a errand for Jesus so I made no face about it.

I said to the mother of that hurt first baseman that we come to see her daughter. I felt like a low-down worm even being in the same room with that poor suffering lady, and with Shazam right beside me not making any sorry face or nothing.

I said to the 2 ladies, "I'm real sorry that bad thing happened to Aki." I did not speak for Shazam.

Those poor people had no doors on some of their cupboards, it was a pitiful shame. And their linoleum was tore away in places, the floorboards showed through. Everything neat as a pin in their yard and their kitchen but I could tell they was down on their luck.

Mrs. Mikami did not show on her face how she recognized Shazam but she must of. She smiled real pleasant and said it was nice of us to come over and she said into a doorway, "Aki, two girls are here to visit you," and she made with her arm like we should go right in.

First I saw the flowers. I never saw so many different bouquets in one room before. There was blue flowers and orange ones and pink and many white ones, and red and yellow too, they was in jars everywhere, even a milk can full of tall velvety cattails standing on the floor beside the bed.

And then I saw Aki. I had been told she had a head and neck brace on her that she had to wear for 3 months but I did not expect such a sight. It was leather and metal like to hold her head rigid and it was huge. I could hardly see her face inside.

And Darlene had told me Aki couldn't talk, so I was not surprised she had a notebook on her lap to write notes on.

Shazam

Manny made me walk in the room with all flowers all over there was that Jap girl sitting in bed I couldnt see her face so much steel all around her.

Manzanita

Shazam had her stare on. She gawked at that poor first baseman like in a zoo. I pointed her to the chair and I stayed standing aside her. I said, "My name is Manzanita, this here is Shazam."

The girl in the bed wrote on her spiral notebook, "HI," in big letters and turned it real slow for us to see.

"Say hi, Shazam," I poked her.

"Hi," she said, sounding like she wanted to unsay it. She kept staring.

"We come to see how you are," I said. This is not exactly the truth. I was telling so many lies for God, I had lost count.

"I'm OK," this girl wrote on the notebook page.

"That's nice," I say. This is not what I meant to say. I

meant to say how sorry I am. How horrible it is. How ashamed us Barlow girls are for what that miserable girl did, how mad we feel on account of we was taken in by her for so long. I meant to say it was none of our fault.

And then I knew why Jesus sent me here. He sent me here to show me how it *was* my fault. How every time I was mean to anyone, even mean to a skunk or raccoon in the garbage, or any time I was rude back to a stinker boy that was rude first — I was making more meanheartedness in the world. And a crazy child like Shazam, born with no married parents to bless her in her life — she seen the meanhearted example set by all the bad people in the world and she just followed along on account of she did not have any morals guidance, it was not even her fault.

"We hope you get that thing off your head real soon, Aki," I said.

"Not for a while yet," she wrote.

It was now or never. I said, "Shazam here has something to say." I did not know if she did or not.

Aki

The girl who hit me with her elbow sat there looking at me and then away from me and back again. I could tell she was unusual.

I remembered that she hadn't shaken my hand in the line on the day of the Bat. I remembered that very clearly. And how embarrassed I was about something I can't help. I can't help looking the way I look.

And then that girl said something.

"You hurt bad?" she asked me.

That was her question. What did she think?

I wrote "I'm all right, it's not so bad." The same thing I'd said to everybody. As I turned the notebook around so the girls could read it, I noticed the word I'd written. "right." It was the same word as always but it suddenly looked different.

How many times had I written it, with all the people who had been coming to see me for so many weeks?

Could I say the truth about it to that girl? How could I do that? It would be so rude.

But I wasn't all right. My head was in a brace that the doctor wouldn't take off for five more weeks. I hadn't brushed my teeth since the morning of the game. People had to feed me through a straw. I hadn't said a word out loud in nearly two months. My head hurt with a dull constant ache from the brace or from something else, nobody knew what. I couldn't go bike riding, I couldn't even play jacks. I had to sit still. My father even cried one night, I heard him standing in the doorway when he thought I was asleep. My own father. I didn't move. He never found out I knew.

But still, I wasn't crippled, and I wasn't dead. That was something to be thankful for.

I had shown Peggy how to write *Shikata ga nai.*

But that was before. I wasn't in the same room with that girl who hit me. Now she was sitting on a chair four feet away from me. And she had asked me if I hurt bad.

How could she ask such an innocent question?

Manzanita

I knew Japanese people was polite but this beat all. Here this girl sits not able to move hardly a muscle and she tells Shazam she's all right.

Shazam

I readed all them words she wrote but not the long one it had a G and a H she said its not bad.

Aki

Could I say the truth? No. I couldn't do that.

Manzanita

If Aki was just going to be nice and polite about it Shazam would not repent which she needed to do. It was real quiet in that room.

Shazam

That was a real big thing on her head.

Aki

Rude as it would be, I thought to try saying it on my notebook page.

Manzanita

It seemed like a bad idea to come here. It was not doing any good.

Aki

How could I do such a rude thing? I decided to do it anyway.

Manzanita

Aki wrote: *Yes, I am hurt badly.* I never saw no more pretty cursive from somebody just going into 7th even though her hand was shaking pretty bad. Now Shazam could see the true truth and we was getting somewhere.

Shazam

Then there was more words to read on that page she wrote it was Yes and some other words I saw the word hurt she was hurt bad.

Aki

My heart jumped in its place, a sudden inflation, and began to pound all through me from the rudeness of what I had just written. That girl really didn't know. Some surprise came into her face, her mouth. She looked all around the room, everywhere except at me.

Manzanita

I was tempted to say something because of the quiet there with just a fly going from the windowsill to the bedstead to the bed cover to Shazam's chair to a jar of zinnias on the floor. I could of said something to make that silence go away. But I didn't.

Shazam

She gots that big thing on her head of leather and metal parts.

Manzanita

I kept waiting.

Aki

I thought about writing, "It's OK, it's not so bad." It would make my heart stop beating like a drum in my throat.

Manzanita

I almost had a case of nerves just being in that room with hundreds of flowers and that fly in the quiet and who could know what was going on in Shazam's crooked mind?

And then I got so mad at her in that silent buzzing room, I wanted to wring her neck. It *wasn't* my fault like I thought a minute ago. I did not set Shazam no bad example.

It's like Audrey said way last winter: Crumptillions of children had fathers die in the war and they're normal people in despite of it.

They don't go jamming their elbows into people's heads.

And there is other children born out of wedding lock. They are not crazy just because of it. God wouldn't make them crazy just to punish their sinful mom and dad.

Shazam

That thing was a head brace.

Aki

My loud heart was frightening. I could have written "It's OK." I didn't. Not even to make my heart be quiet. I had been so rude and yet I didn't take it back. It was the truth.

Manzanita

That fly buzzed onto Aki's face. She brushed at it with a slow motion of her hand.

Shazam sat there with her lipped-in face.

I was near ready to scream, I had my teeth gritted in that speechless room.

Shazam

Her face was way inside that head thing I seen her eyes look at me.

Aki

Or I could write "Thanks for coming."

Shazam

Her face a Jap face.

Manzanita

That girl Aki would hate me in seventh grade for bringing this silent crazy person to her very own private bedroom. I could never make it up to her.

Shazam

That girl did not move her head.

Manzanita

I thought how I must of done wrong bringing her here. She wasn't catching on no more than a stick. And that grandmother had bowed to her! I could of screamed. I held on and listened to that fly go around the room, across my face and over to Shazam and back to the window again.

Shazam

Jap airplanes bombed my fathers ship fire everywhere I couldnt breathe nobody could get out.

Aki

That girl kept staring at me. I looked up at Manzanita standing there, apologizing to me with her face. My heart wouldn't quiet down.

Manzanita

God couldn't be wrong about this, but I sure was tempted to think so. Be of good courage, Manny.

Aki

My grandmother brought in three glasses of lemonade on a tray and offered them to the two girls, who took them. Manzanita said, "Thank you." Then my grandmother sat on my bed and put the straw from my glass in my mouth. It was really good lemonade.

I hadn't brushed my teeth for all those weeks. It was disgusting.

When I'd had a few drinks I put my hand up to show my grandmother that was enough. She got up off my bed and went back into the kitchen.

Shazam

My mom she said over and over again. My stomach squeezed it hurted so bad. We had to have gas masks so when they bomb us again.

Manzanita

Even my friends were not so friendly when I had my spells of seeing Jesus, this time for sure they would not like me for what I done bringing this awful thing to pass.

Shazam

I ran to first base that Jap face there.

Aki

I nearly got my pencil in writing position to say "It's OK." I almost did.

Manzanita

I could not be of good courage much longer. The minutes was going by.

Shazam

I ran into her. That big thing on her head that fly buzz I guess Im sorry.

Aki

I nearly had the pencil on the page. And then that peculiar girl said, "I'm sorry."

Manzanita

Praise God.

Aki

Now I could write "It's OK" or "Thanks for coming." I still didn't do it. I just didn't.

Shazam

My stomach squeezed I stood up Manny come with me.

Manzanita

I didn't know what God wanted me to do now but I felt we had to quit while we was ahead. Me and Aki looked at each other and I hoped she could see my feelings of how sorry I was she had to sit there all that silent time and how I was praising God Shazam finally got a brain in her head to do the decent thing.

Shazam was almost out the door and I said to Aki, "We better go now."

Aki

Now I wrote "Thanks for coming." Manzanita said she was glad they came. That other girl kept her eyes on the door. They left. My heart still kept telling me I had been rude. But I knew too I had been right.

Manzanita

The road to Barlow is mostly downhill and we coasted. I told Shazam she done the right thing. In my heart I found out I was actually starting to like her. Or like some little part of her.

Shazam did not say much. Once she said how good Brita Marie's bike rode. And once she said her stomach hurt. I told her it must of been something she ate. She didn't say anything more.

We passed them absent-minded cows in the field above the Flying Horse gas station with their easy lives, they don't have right and wrong. I was jealous of them for a moment and then I took it back. They don't have no possibility of choosing anything, only just which grass they'll eat, at the right or left of their heads.

When we rode past the men sitting on the porch at the Barlow General Store they looked up, but I did not even wave like I usually do. Let them discuss how that disgrace of a girl was out joyriding on Brita Marie's bike, I didn't care. I was too full of complication of what-all happened at Aki's house.

Ever since, Jesus never once come to me telling me I done a good job. I wish he would of.

Shazam

I keep my puka shells on that palm tree silk scarf all ready to fold up take with if they make me go away. I keep putting up that fence keep the deer out its hard work the sun too hot.

That Jap girl hurt bad. I hurt her with my arm.

They thought I would go back with my mom I got the stomach squeeze. They said I would go back with her then they said I would not.

My grammama gets her headaches I can fry the bacon up myself. I took her a bacon sandwich in her bed she said thank you dear. It is a name she says to me.

Tootie

I lost my pep. Even my mom said, "I never hear you say Hubba hubba ding ding anymore." I did not feel like hubba hubba ding ding anymore.

One day after berrypicking I got some girls and we rode our bikes down to the Flying Horse gas station where that man has the board with all the Bat 6 scores on it. I got Ellen, Daisy, and Vernell, and Daisy's friend Wink from Barlow said she would meet us there, and when she got there she had their catcher, Audrey, with her, because it is Audrey's great-uncle Beau that puts the scores up every year. Lorelei could not go because she had to thin apples for her dad.

The year 1949 was a blank on the board.

We parked our bikes and went over to where he was spraying the dust down with the hose.

Audrey said hello first, and she said, "This is my great-uncle Beau." Then all of us from the Ridge told our names.

"We were wondering what you're gonna put up on the board for 1949," she said. Just hearing that made me mad all over again.

He looked at all 6 of us gathered there and he said, "That was a sad day, I don't know what to write."

"Well, what do you *think* you're going to put on it?" I asked.

"Well, I just don't know," he said.

Then Ellen said, "How about just the names of the two teams?"

Here it was August and I was resentful to admit the truth of it, there would be no MVP for 1949. Not even a score.

"I don't think a blank 1949 would be very nice," said Vernell.

And that Beau looked down at her and he got her point. "I get your point, it wouldn't be very nice, would it?" he said.

"Could you put the names of the teams?" said Daisy. "And just leave it like that? So at least our children won't have to look at just a blank space?"

Beau said he thought that would be a good idea, and he went inside the station and climbed up the ladder to a high shelf way above the rows of fan belts, and he got small cans of red and green paint and he got 2 brushes from a drawer. And he painted the team names while we watched. The tall Barlow first baseman held the 2 cans of paint for him.

Watching it made my heart sink all over again.

But there is one thing. We lived through it. That is something.

Shazam

Out there by the woods Shig put his arm out front Stop I looked he pointed a deer leaping high over 3 logs come down thunder on the ground I never saw no such big jump. Shig whispered pretty huh I whispered yes.

Alva

Dear God,

I still don't understand. Even with Manny being so free-hearted to take that awful girl to face up to the first baseman she hurt so bad. I still don't get it at all.

If You know everything, why don't You let us understand?

Wink thought Shazam was sent here to test our Christian goodness. But I don't get that either.

And also I don't understand why Shazam couldn't go back to her mother. Why do we have to have her with us in 7th? How much Christian goodness do we have to learn?

I feel sorry for the sixth graders coming up, they will not have Mrs. Winters, she is having her baby. Did she get too sad with what happened and she doesn't want to teach anybody anymore?

Thy will be done.

Your friend,
Alva

CONNECTIONS

from Farewell to Manzanar

Jeanne Wakatsuki Houston
and
James D. Houston

How do you think Aki felt when she was forced to leave her home and travel to an internment camp? The following excerpt, from a memoir by a Japanese American author who had an experience similar to Aki's, gives us an idea of what Aki's trip and her first night at the camp might have been like.

I had never been outside Los Angeles County, never traveled more than ten miles from the coast, had never even ridden on a bus. I was full of excitement, the way any kid would be, and wanted to look out the window. But for the first few hours the shades were drawn. Around me other people played cards, read magazines, dozed, waiting. I settled back, waiting too, and finally fell asleep. The bus felt very secure to me. Almost half its passengers were immediate relatives. Mama and my older brothers had succeeded in keeping most of us together, on the same bus, headed for the same camp. I didn't realize until much later what a job that was. The strategy had been, first, to have everyone living in the same district when the evacuation began, and then to get all of us included under the same family number, even though names had been changed by marriage. Many families weren't as lucky as ours and suffered months of anguish while trying to arrange transfers from one camp to another.

We rode all day. By the time we reached our destination, the shades were up. It was late afternoon. The first thing I saw was a yellow swirl across a blurred, reddish setting sun. The bus was being pelted by what sounded like splattering rain. This was my first look at something I would soon know very well, a billowing flurry of dust and sand churned up by the wind through Owens Valley.

We drove past a barbed-wire fence, through a gate, and into an open space where trunks and sacks and packages had been dumped from the baggage trucks that drove out ahead of us. I could see a few tents set up, the first rows of black barracks, and beyond them, blurred by sand, rows of barracks that seemed to spread for miles across this plain. People were sitting on cartons or milling around, with their backs to the wind, waiting to see which friends or relatives might be on this bus. As we approached, they turned or stood up, and some moved toward us expectantly. But inside the bus no one stirred. no one waved or spoke. They just stared out the windows, ominously silent. I didn't understand this. Hadn't we finally arrived, our whole family intact? I opened a window, leaned out, and yelled happily. "Hey! This whole bus is full of Wakatsukis!"

Outside, the greeters smiled. Inside there was an explosion of laughter, hysterical, tension-breaking laughter that left my brothers choking and whacking each other across the shoulders.

We had pulled up just in time for dinner. The mess halls weren't completed yet. An outdoor chow line snaked around a half-finished building that broke a good part of the wind. They issued us army mess kits, the round metal kind that fold over, and plopped in scoops of canned Vienna sausage, canned string beans, steamed rice that had been cooked too long, and on top of the rice a serving of canned apricots. The Caucasian servers were thinking that the fruit poured over rice would make a good dessert. Among the Japanese, of course, rice is never eaten with sweet foods, only with salty or savory foods. Few of us could eat such a mixture. But at this point no one dared protest. It would have been impolite. I was horrified when I saw the apricot syrup seeping through my little mound of rice. I opened my mouth to complain. My mother jabbed me in the back to keep quiet. We moved on through the line and joined the other squatting in the lee of half-raised walls, dabbing courteously at what was, for almost everyone there, an inedible concoction.

After dinner we were taken to Block 16, a cluster of fifteen barracks that had just been finished a day or so earlier—although finished was hardly the word for it. The shacks were built of one thickness of pine planking covered with tarpaper. They sat on concrete footings, with about two feet of open space between the floorboards and the ground. Gaps showed between the planks, and as the weeks passed and the green wood dried out, the gaps widened. Knotholes gaped in the uncovered floor.

Each barracks was divided into six units, sixteen by twenty feet, about the size of a living room, with one bare bulb hanging from the ceiling and an oil stove for heat. We were assigned two of these for the twelve people in our family group; and our official family "number" was enlarged by three digits—16 plus the number of this barracks. We were issued steel army cots, two brown army blankets each, and some mattress covers, which my brothers stuffed with straw.

The first task was to divide up what space we had for sleeping. Bill and Woody contributed a blanket each and partitioned off the first room: one side for Bill and Tomi, one side for Woody and Chizu and their baby girl. Woody also got the stove, for heating formulas.

The people who had it hardest during the first few months were young couples like these, many of whom had married just before the evacuation began, in order to not be separated and sent to different camps. Our two rooms were crowded, but at least it was all in the family. My oldest sister and her husband were shoved into one of those sixteen-by-twenty-foot compartments with six people they had never seen before—two other couples, one recently married like themselves, the other with two teenage boys. Partitioning off a room like that wasn't easy. It was bitter cold when we arrived, and the wind did not abate. All they had to use for room dividers were those army blankets, two of which were barely enough to keep one person warm. They argued over whose blanket should be sacrificed and later argued about noise at night—the parents wanted their boys asleep by 9:00 P.M.— and they continued arguing over matters like that for six months, until my sister and her husband left to harvest sugar beets in Idaho. It was grueling work up there, and wages were pitiful, but when the call came through camp for workers to alleviate the wartime labor shortage, it sounded better than their life at Manzanar. They knew they'd have, if nothing else, a room, perhaps a cabin of their own.

That first night in Block 16, the rest of us squeezed into the second room—Granny, Lillian, age fourteen, Ray, thirteen, May, eleven, Kiyo, ten, Mama, and me. I didn't mind this at all at the time. Being youngest meant I got to sleep with Mama. And before we went to bed I had a great time jumping up and down on the mattress. The boys had stuffed so much straw into hers, we had to flatten it some so we wouldn't slide off. I slept with her every night after that until Papa came back.

■   ■   ■

The Battle, Over and Over Again
(given as testimony in support of the student's case against racism at columbia university)
Safiya Henderson-Holmes

Unlike Bat 6, *this poem is told from the perspective of a mother of a young girl who is a victim of prejudice. Aki's parents probably felt a similar mixture of helplessness and frustration after Aki was attacked at the softball game.*

my daughter came home from school one day
when she was four
she ran into the bathroom, crying and
sitting on the floor

i said,—baby, what's the matter, c'mon,
what could be so bad
i bought you a box of cherry fun fruits,
bet that'll make you glad—

she lifted up her little arms, squinted in the light
mommy, she asked,—why didn't god make me white—

she dropped her arms and question hard on her lap
her eyes were closed, my knees were weak, she said,

—they keep saying i'm ugly, and they say
it's because i'm black—
the bathroom had always been our place we ran to
whenever she was hurt

we'd band-aid the cuts, pull out the splinters
and wash away the dirt
but suddenly our refuge had become a place for war

with bombs waiting to explode
the sink's faucet dripped like a timer,
the pipes signaled an enemy code

who said these things, i wanted to ask,
but i didn't let out the words
my child picking away her dark brown skin
had loosened every nerve

and who was not important, more important was the why
that in 1983 america, racism was making my child cry

i sat beside her on the floor, pulled her to my chest
i thought of how often we had sat like this
just to take a rest

—sweetheart—i said,—now you know you're not ugly—
i pasted words in the air,

—you're one of the prettiest girls i've ever seen, anywhere—
her back was warm and sweaty, she held her muscles tight

there was sand on her cheeks,
she was much too young to fight
the air was full of bullet holes, i could smell the dead

—and you have the prettiest smile—
my daughter shook her head
i pushed against the bathroom wall,
trying to gain a balance

trying to find the perfect words
to break this painful silence
i thought of all the great ones
who had died to prevent such a day

the fannie lous, malcolms,[1]
name calling dragons that they slayed
i thought about the marches,
shouts of let freedom ring

busrides, boycotts, sit-ins, speeches, endless praying
the world stood boldly in my bathroom,
between my child and me

and i wondered as i squeezed her hands,
how long will the battle be
her eyes opened and looked in mine,
as if she heard my fear

she hugged my neck and said,—mommy, i don't care
they're two mean boys and they're always starting fights
they never have anything special for lunch,
they always ask for bites—
she straightened and coughed,
her arms still around my neck

---

1. Fannie Lou Hamer (1917–1977) and Malcolm X (1925–1965) were African American civil rights activists.

—and i'm going to take my fun fruits to school,
and they won't get a peck—
she said,—and the bigger one is going to ask
until his face gets red—

she wiped her eyes, rubbed sand from her head
pointed to her left arm, swallowed and said,

—one thing i know,—
she placed her hands on her hips,
i saw her strength begin to grow

—mommy, his face gets like that when he's mad,
i seen it lots of times
mommy, i think his face is more ugly than mine—

i kissed her softly on her mouth, both her sandy cheeks,
washed her face, and studied the draining water
as if it were the last enemy's retreat

■ ■ ■

The Frog-King, or Iron Henry

Jakob and Wilhelm Grimm

In Bat 6, *the Japanese Americans living in Barlow and Bear Creek Ridge were considered to be dangerous just because of the way they looked. Like* Bat 6, *this German folk tale suggests that it is unwise to judge people on such a narrow basis, since things are often very different than they appear.*

In old times when wishing still helped one, there lived a king whose daughters were all beautiful, but the youngest was so beautiful that the sun itself, which has seen so much, was astonished whenever it shone in her face. Close by the King's castle lay a great dark forest, and under an old lime-tree in the forest was a well, and when the day was very warm, the King's child went out into the forest and sat down by the side of the cool fountain, and when she was dull she took a golden ball, and threw it up on high and caught it, and this ball was her favourite plaything.

Now it so happened that on one occasion the princess' golden ball did not fall into the little hand which she was holding up for it, but on to the ground beyond, and rolled straight into the water. The King's daughter followed it with her eyes, but it vanished, and the well was deep, so deep that the bottom could not be seen. On this she began to cry, and cried louder and louder, and could not be comforted. And as she thus lamented, someone said to her, "What ails thee, King's daughter? Thou weepest so that even a stone would show pity." She looked round to the side from whence the voice came, and saw a frog stretching forth its thick, ugly head from the water. "Ah! old water-splasher, is it thou?" said she; "I am weeping for my golden ball, which has fallen into the well."

"Be quiet, and do not weep," answered the frog. "I can help thee, but what wilt thou give me if I bring thy play-thing up again?" "Whatever thou wilt have, dear frog," said she—"my clothes, my pearls and jewels, and even the golden crown which I am wearing."

The frog answered, "I do not care for thy clothes, thy pearls and jewels, or thy golden crown, but if thou wilt love me and let me be thy companion and play-fellow, and sit by thee at thy little table, and eat off thy little golden plate, and drink out of thy little cup, and sleep in thy little bed— if thou wilt promise me this I will go down below, and bring thee thy golden ball up again."

"Oh, yes," said she, "I promise thee all thou wishest, if thou wilt but bring me my ball back again." She, however, thought, "How silly the frog does talk! He lives in the water with the other frogs and croaks, and can be no companion to any human being!"

But the frog when he had received this promise put his head into the water and sank down, and in a short time came swimming up again with the ball in his mouth, and threw it on the grass. The King's daughter was delighted to see her pretty plaything once more, and picked it up, and ran away with it. "Wait, wait," said the frog. "Take me with thee. I can't run as thou canst." But what did it avail him to scream his croak, croak, after her, as loudly as he could? She did not listen to it, but ran home and soon forgot the poor frog, who was forced to go back into his well again.

The next day when she had seated herself at table with the King and all the courtiers, and was eating from her little golden plate, something came creeping splish, splash, splish, splash, up the marble staircase, and when it had got to the top, it knocked at the door and cried, "Princess, youngest princess, open the door for me." She ran to see who was outside, but when she opened the door, there sat the frog in front of it. Then she slammed the door to, in great haste, sat down to dinner again, and was quite frightened. The King saw plainly that her heart was beating violently, and said, "My child, what art thou so afraid of? Is there perchance a giant outside who wants to carry thee away?" "Ah, no," replied she, "it is no giant, but a disgusting frog."

"What does the frog want with thee?" "Ah, dear father, yesterday when I was in the forest sitting by the well, playing, my golden ball fell into the water. And because I cried so, the frog brought it out again for me, and because he insisted so on it, I promised him he should be my companion, but I never thought he would be able to come out of his water! And now he is outside there, and wants to come in to me."

In the meantime it knocked a second time, and cried,
"Princess! youngest princess!
Open the door for me!
Dost thou not know what thou saidst to me
Yesterday by the cool waters of the fountain?
Princess, youngest princess!
Open the door for me!"

Then said the King, "That which thou hast promised, must thou perform. Go and let him in." She went and opened the door, and the frog hopped in and followed her, step by step, to her chair. There he sat still and cried, "Lift me up beside thee." She delayed, until at last the King commanded her to do it. When the frog was once on the chair he wanted to be on the table, and when he was on the table he said, "Now, push thy tiny little golden plate nearer to me that we may eat together." She did this, but it was easy to see that she did not do it willingly. The frog enjoyed what he ate, but almost every mouthful she took choked her. At length he said, "I have eaten and am satisfied; now I am tired, carry me into thy little room and make thy little silken bed ready, and we will both lie down and go to sleep."

The King's daughter began to cry, for she was afraid of the cold frog which she did not like to touch, and which was not to sleep in her pretty, clean little bed. But the King grew angry and said, "He who helped thee when thou wert in trouble ought not afterwards to be despised by thee." So she took hold of the frog with two fingers, carried him upstairs, and put him in a corner. But when she was in bed he crept to her and said, "I am tired, I want to sleep as well as thou, lift me up or I will tell thy father." Then she was terribly angry, and took him up and threw him with all her might against the wall. "Now, thou wilt be quiet, odious frog," said she. But when he fell down he was no frog but a King's son with beautiful, kind eyes. He by her father's will was now her dear companion and husband. Then he told her how he had been bewitched by a wicked witch, and how no one could have delivered him from the well but herself, and that to-morrow they would go together to his kingdom. Then they went to sleep, and next morning when the sun awoke them, a carriage came driving up with eight white horses, which had white ostrich feathers on their heads, and were harnessed with golden chains, and behind stood the young King's servant, Faithful Henry. Faithful Henry had been so unhappy when his master was changed into a frog, that he had caused three iron bands to be laid round his heart, lest it should burst with grief and sadness. The carriage was to conduct the young King into his kingdom. Faithful Henry helped them both in, and placed himself behind again, and was full of joy because of this deliverance. And when they had driven a part of the way, the King's son heard a cracking behind him as if something had broken. So he turned round and cried, "Henry, the carriage is breaking."

"No master, it is not the carriage. It is a band from my heart, which was put there in my great pain when you were a frog and imprisoned in the well." Again and once again while they were on their way something cracked, and each time the King's son thought the carriage was breaking; but it was only the bands which were springing from the heart of Faithful Henry because his master was set free and was happy.

■ ■ ■

Like Japanese Americans during WWII, Hispanic Americans have been accused of disloyalty to their country simply because of their ancestry. In this poem by an unknown author, which was published in 1898 on the eve of the Spanish-American War, the speaker defends Hispanic Americans from the many "opinions" against them. The poem makes an argument that could equally apply to Japanese Americans in the 1940s.

La voz del hispano

Muchas son las opinones
En contra del pueblo hispano,
Y le acusan de traidor
Al gobierno americano

Haciendo un experimento,
Quedarán desengañados,
Que nuestros bravos nativos
No rehusan ser soldados,

No importa lo que se diga
Y difame de su fama,
Pero pelearán gustosos
Por el águila americana,

A nuestro pueblo nativo
Le acusan de ser canalla,
Pero no ha demostrado serlo,
En el campo de batalla….

Como buenos compatriotas
Y fieles americanos,
Libraremos de ese yugo
A los humildes cubanos…

The Voice of the Hispano

Many are the opinions
Against the Hispanic people
And they accuse them of betraying
The American government.

Making an experiment
They will be disillusioned,
Our brave native men
Do not refuse to be soldiers.

It matters not what is said
Or how our fame is insulted,
As they will fight with pleasure
For the American eagle.

They accuse our native people
Of being rabble,
But they have not proven to be so
On the battlefield.

Like good countrymen
And faithful Americans,
We will free from that yoke
The humble Cubans.

■ ■ ■

Virginia Euwer Wolff

(1937–)

Virginia Euwer Wolff says three things have profoundly influenced her life: growing up in the Pacific Northwest, playing the violin, and the death of her father when she was young. "I'm also five foot three and very ordinary looking," she says. "My background is probably pretty average."

Wolff may have a self-described ordinary background, but her varied interests, exceptional talent with the English language, and sometimes painfully honest sensitivity to human nature have allowed her to create some extraordinary fiction for young adults. Her father, a lawyer, and her mother, a teacher, were also farmers who lived in Oregon, where Wolff was born in 1937. Wolff herself has two children, and she now lives in her home state. In addition to being a violinist, she has been a swimming teacher and a lifeguard, and she has taught high school English at an academy for highly competitive snow skiers.

Wolff began teaching school in 1959. A lifelong teacher, she has worked with young people of all ages, from kindergartners to college students, and enjoys teaching students of all ages. Because Wolff's research for her novels comes from watching, listening, and simply wandering around, it is inevitable that her writing is filled with students, teachers, and schools. Her first young adult novel, *Probably Still Nick Swansen,* is the story of a learning-disabled boy and his experiences at school. A more recent novel, *Make Lemonade,* explores the difference that exceptional teachers can make to students who are struggling to improve their lives. In fact, years in the classroom have given Wolff a deep respect for teachers and especially those dedicated teachers who go far beyond what is expected of them.

In the late 1970s, even though she had never taken a writing class, Wolff started writing. She boldly decided to write a novel, though she had never even finished a short story. Wolff acknowledges that a number of her teachers guided her toward making the decision to become a writer. She also singles out the great American writer William Faulkner as a major influence on her work. She explains, "Faulkner said these are the only things worth writing about: love, honor, pity, pride, compassion, and sacrifice. These things constitute the moral checklist against which I place my work."

■ ■ ■